DEDICATION

To all those "Gaijins" who live and work in Japan . . . and to the Japanese people who so patiently put up with us.

Son of Raw Fish

By Don Maloney

The **Japan Times**, Ltd.

First Edition: February 1977
Second Printing: July 1977
Third Printing: February 1978

Cover and art work: Koji Detake

Published by

The **Japan Times**, Ltd.

5-4, Shibaura 4-chome, Minato-ku,
Tokyo, 108, Japan

Printed in Japan

CONTENTS

FOREWORD   by Toshio Matsuoka   8
PREFACE   11

I.   THE LANGUAGE   14
     What's in a Name?   16
     Japanese is Not My Cup of Tea   19
     Yes, It *Isn't* an Easy Language   22
     Kore wa Toiretto Peipaa Desu   25
     It's Bread There Isn't Any of   28
     Back to Japanese Lessons, Desho?   31
     Don't Just Sit There   34

II. TRAVEL   38
     Row, Row, Row Your Boat   40
     No Frills   43
     They Enjoyed Having Me   46
     Yes, Sarah, There Is a Narita Airport   50
     Maybe the Party's Over   53
     Sea for Yourself   56
     Not with a Roar, But a Whimper   59

III. HOME LIFE   64
     Cockroaches—There, I Said It   66
     You Don't Know Me   69
     Hands Off   73
     Smoking Is a Drag   76
     2.2 Pounds per Kilo   79
     Iced Tea—On the Rocks   82
     Just Once I'd Like to See   85

Here Comes the Judge 88
Something Old, Something New 91
For Better or for Worse 94
Please Buy the Book 98
How's the Book Going? 100

IV. LEISURE LIFE 104
Accentuate the Positive 106
Don't Go near the Water 109
A Modern Tale of Genji 112
Mafia-San 117
Dead Giveaway 120
Good Evening; It's Morning 123

V. BUSINESS IS BUSINESS 128
The Yen is Up Because It's Down 130
Yamamoto's Rules of Order 133
More About Meetings 136
Poverty Begins at Home 139
Free Advice—It's Always Worth It 143
Yankee Doodle Still Wants to Go to London 146

VI. HOLIDAYS 150
Happy New Year, Your Majesty 152
July Fourth Thanksgiving Day? 155
One of Those Days 157
Yes, Virginia, There Is a Mt. Fuji 161
Good News, Bad News 164

VII. THE REAL JAPAN 168
Why Don't They Name the Streets? 170
A Little Womb Music, Maestro 173

Tokyo Has Its Ups and Downs 176
Present Imperfect 179
Shine on Harvest Moon 182
Kyoto Revisited 186
I'm the Person Who Eats 189
Give and You Shall Receive 191

VIII. GOING HOME 198
Home Is the Place Where 200
747's That Pass in the Night 203
Sayonara! 206

AFTERWORD 213

7

FOREWORD

Yukio Mishima once wrote to the effect that Japan and America are very similar — in the sense that both countries care about their reputation abroad. But I myself think they are very distinct in the way they care.

Americans as a nation may be pleased or upset at the praise or criticism they receive abroad. But rarely do they ask (or care) as individuals what others think about them. The Japanese, however, feel deeply self-conscious as individuals about what others think of them and their country.

If you've ever been to Japan you will know what I mean. The first question you're bound to hear is: "What do you think of Japan?" or "What do you think of the Japanese?" I lived for three years in New York and never once had such questions asked me about America.

The concern is not only on the part of Japanese leaders. Even ordinary Japanese are worried about what others think of Japan. Perhaps that is one reason they so avidly grab up books on Japan with titles such as *Foreigners' Views of Japan, The Japanese Through Blue Eyes,* or *Theories on the Japanese* authored by people from other lands.

It was not strange then that when Don Maloney's first book, *Japan: It's Not All Raw Fish,* was translated into Japanese as *Gaijin wa Tsurai Yo!* and published jointly by The Japan Times and PHP Institute, it hit the bestseller lists in Japan.

One of the reasons it did so well, no doubt, was that it was a "people to people" book. Most of the books on Japan are written by foreigners who speak Japanese fluently and who are well-versed in Japanese history and literature. Though excellently done and contributing greatly to international understanding, you can imagine that they were written in a library or scholar's study and addressed to university people or serious students of Japan.

Not so Maloney's. He playfully claims (always joking!) that only other Americans who've studied in the same class at the same school can understand the Japanese he spent ¥6 million to learn. But he did something no one else had ever done. He spoke as an ordinary person about things that happened to him in *daily life* in Japan — ordinary things that almost everybody could understand and identify with.

He didn't presume that he had seen all of Japan or the lives of all the Japanese. He didn't even say he had experienced all the things all foreigners experience in Japan. He just wanted to tell others what happened to him.

His ideas came to him in elevators, department stores and company meeting rooms. He wrote in hotels and offices, riding the "bullet train" and seated at the dining table in his noisy home situated in a Japanese neighborhood. He didn't write about politics or Zen, temples or Mt. Fuji — though before he came to Japan he had been well-prepared for them. Instead he wrote about the ordinary things — for which he had been totally unprepared!

Because he wrote of language problems, misunderstandings, high food costs, mannerisms and noises, many foreigners criticized him and told him curtly, "If you don't like Japan, why don't you leave?" As for the Japanese, his blunt words shocked, and earned for him the nickname "Mr. Kado ga Tatsu" (Mr. Harsh)!

I must admit that at first I shared their sentiments. But

9

then I came to know Don Maloney well, and realized that he was not complaining, nor even demanding that anyone agree. He did want people to understand, though, and believed that only frankness, not flattery, could provide the insight necessary. He wanted foreigners to be prepared for the thousand little things that make up life in Japan — which if not understood can cause real trouble. He wanted the Japanese to be aware of how some foreigners might be taking things, and of how many "taken for granted" things might not be clear at all to foreigners.

I know for one that he enabled us to appreciate much that we didn't realize about ourselves.

Someone once said that working for international understanding is like scooping up the waters of the Pacific with a teacup. If that is true, then Don Maloney's "cup" is as huge as he is, for I think he has done (and in this book continues to do) a great deal for the understanding of Japan.

Toshio Matsuoka

10

PREFACE

For a little more than nine months now, I — along with Wife Sarah and Son Donald — have been groping our ways through the Reverse Cultural Shock brought about by our return to Cleveland.

It hasn't been an easy task for any of us.

In fact — although those of you still in Japan and still trying to learn your "Migi" from your "Hidari" are going to find this impossible to believe — coming home is far more difficult than trying to get with it in Tokyo.

For one thing, when we went to Tokyo, we *knew* we were in a foreign country — as foreign as a country can be. So, we were ready for the shock. And, Japan provided plenty of them. Right up to the day we left.

But, coming back to Cleveland — we thought, anyway — was to be quite a different story. After all, it *was* home.

At least, my passport says it's home. I hope the passport is right — soon. But, as I write this, I'm more thoroughly "Gaijin" in Cleveland than I ever was in Tokyo.

There are unmistakable signs, however, that I'm coming around. For instance, I've stopped kicking off my shoes when Wife Sarah and I go visiting. And, I'm resigned to the fact that no round-trips to Hong Kong are given away at Son Donald's school PTA dances. I no longer feel that I'm going to get arrested for grand larceny when I pay only a dollar for three or four melons. Plus, it's been weeks now since I last yelled "Sumimasen" to get a waiter's attention.

Why, I don't even remember the last time I pushed a "door close" button in a Cleveland elevator.

11

If you've read any of my Japan Times "Never the Twain . . ." columns, or heard me do an MC job at any of the Japan banquets, or read even part of my first book ("Japan: It's Not All Raw Fish"), then you know how often I found myself a victim of the chaos that is Tokyo for a bumbling foreigner like me.

And, if you've lived in Japan for at least six hours, you know that every word I wrote about Gaijin life there was true.

I really planned that my second book would be about what happens to former "Gaijins in Japan" when they return home. In fact, I wrote it. But, friends and relatives who read the copy didn't believe a word. Because, I guess, they never did a hitch in Japan.

So, I decided to do a second book about Japan. And this is it.

Mostly about Japan, anyway, I've included just a couple of excerpts from the almost-was book about the return home.

You will probably recognize all the Japan stories — and, like my mentioned friends and relatives — decide there's no truth to the return-home stories.

Until, at least, you go back home yourself.

Don Maloney

Cleveland, January 1977

Son of Raw Fish

By Don Maloney

I. THE LANGUAGE

Let's face it — that famous "Twain" never *will* really meet until either all the Japanese learn English, or until all foreigners learn Japanese.

I know either is possible, since I've watched and listened as some Japanese handled our language quite well. And, I've been around while some show-off foreigner handled a conversation in genuine Japanese that went considerably deeper than "Kore wa hon desu."

But, one thing that I know is *not* possible is that yours truly will ever be certified by Naganuma as an accomplished Japanese linguist. And, to tell you the truth, I'm glad that's the way it is.

Some of the most interesting and entertaining times I enjoyed in Japan would never have happened if I knew what was *really* going on. In a few pages, you'll know what I mean.

WHAT'S IN A NAME?

The time was January 1970.

The place was Cleveland, Ohio.

The scene was the Maloneys'. dining room at suppertime.

The cast included yours truly, Wife Sarah, Daughters Frances and Barbara, and Sons Sean and Donald.

The dialogue went something like this:

Wife Sarah: "Well, what's new at the office?"

Me: "They're sending us to Japan."

Wife Sarah: "You mean your company is giving us a vacation in Japan."

Me: "I wouldn't say *that*. We're going to live there for a couple of years."

All (except me): "LIVE? In Japan?"

Me: "Live. In Japan."

All (except me
again): "For a couple of years?"

Me: "For a couple of years."

Then, for a longer period than usual at suppertimes up until then, *silence.*

Oh, there wasn't *utter* silence. Everybody said things like pass the roast beef or the mashed potatoes and gravy. But what I mean is, there was no more talk about Japan.

Finally, I couldn't stand it any more and started to explain the whys of the move. I told everybody how I was going over to Tokyo and, in two years time or less, learn the language, understand Japanese government regulations and business methods, set up a company there based entirely on proven American principles, get this new company off and running profitably, turn it over to a successor, and come home. (That statement of objectives, by the way, was pronounced almost five years ago. So far, I *have* come to Tokyo.)

16

The kids were not dying to move to Tokyo for much the same reasons as they resisted the move from New York to Cleveland four years before that suppertime. You know, "We don't want to leave our friends." "We don't want to change schools." Etc., etc.

But, I explained as to how I didn't want to change companies any more than they wanted to change schools, so we *were* going to Tokyo.

I always feel sorry for the way kids inevitably lose arguments — or discussions, as Wife Sarah prefers to call them — over major family policy matters. So, when Daughter Barbara — then 12 — asked, "If I come to Tokyo with you, can I have a dog?," I said sure she could.

At this point, Wife Sarah — all for the Tokyo caper up until then — threw out a "Wait just a minute here!"

I knew what was coming because Wife Sarah has never been anxious to have domestic animals of *any* kind in any house she is expected to keep in order. A rather lively "discussion" followed, and we all finally agreed on Tokyo *and* a new dog.

We'd just barely settled down in our Kamikitazawa house in Tokyo and become used to walking around inside with our shoes off when Daughter Barbara reminded us of our canine promise. Wife Sarah sought to reason with her but Barbara maintained "a deal's a deal" attitude, and everybody voted with her.

Wife Sarah, mellowing somewhat, asked if she wouldn't be equally satisfied with some sort of animal that spent its time in a bowl or a cage, and pointed a glorious picture of ownership of bowled and caged pets.

Daughter Barbara stood fast.

With the assistance — Wife Sarah called it collusion — of a Japanese neighbor, we soon acquired a little white Maltese Terrier. It weighed only about a kilo — normal for a slice of

Japanese toast, but small for a dog.

Anyway, then came the problem of naming the dog. I wanted to call it ''Miracle,'' because that's what I thought of the fact that Wife Sarah had allowed it in the house.

But, Daughter Barbara insisted on a real Japanese name, and since it was so small — she christened it ''Sukoshi.''

Now we all thought that was clever. At least, until we started to call the dog by name in public. The Japanese neighbors thought we were crazy. Imagine what you'd think if, back in Cleveland, a Japanese family moved in on the street and called their dog ''A Little Bit.'' That's what ''Sukoshi'' means in Japanese. We thought it meant ''small.''

Worse than that, Daughter Frances took in a cat while she was away at the University of Dayton and brought it to Japan with her last year. Back there, she looked up, in her Japanese-English dictionary, the Japanese word for ''cat'' and found it was ''Neko.'' So, she named the cat ''Neko.'' Sounded cute in Dayton, Ohio, I suppose. In Tokyo, it made us sound completely mad to call a cat ''Neko,'' even if we *did* already a dog ''Sukoshi.''

Worst part of all of this came recently when Daughter Frances returned to the U.S. Because she wanted to make some stops on the way home, I had to ship the cat to her later. You should have been at the freight counter at Tokyo's Haneda Airport when the little girl there was filling out the shipping papers and asked me the cat's name. I told her, and another of those ''only in Japan'' rhubarbs began. After all, she had lived her entire life here and knew cats are called ''Nekos.'' But, she insisted she needed the particular name of this particular neko. I assured her that I knew what she meant, and that this neko was ''Neko.'' And around and around we went.

Finally, when I told her we also had a dog named ''Sukoshi'' at home, she understood.

18

Incidentally, you should know that because Wife Sarah made her pitch about the bowled and caged pets sound so attractive, Son Donald has about a dozen fish and a parakeet.

I'll be damned if I'll tell you *their* names.

JAPANESE IS NOT MY CUP OF TEA

Every once in a while, I'm overcome by a rickshawful of shame when I realize that I've been living and working in Japan for more than five years now and still don't have a firm handle on the local language.

Now and then, I make a self-convincing resolution to correct all that and to start speaking only Japanese to all who will listen. So I'll make mistakes when I do. So what? I reason that those mistakes will help the language-learning process, not hinder it.

But, then what happens?

I'll tell you: The very next day after such a pledge, I find myself in some situation where I hear *another* Gaijin trying *his* hand at the language. You know, I hear one saying ''Wakarimarcus'' or ''Orrigitio Gozayimust'' or something like that. And it hits me. ''Good Lord,'' I think, ''I bet *I* sound just like that.''

And I go back to English.

But, that's not always the answer, either. English, I find more and more every day, gets me into as much or more trouble than Japanese.

Especially when I'm talking to a Japanese who has faked me into believing that he understands English.

Like the other day, I was about a half-hour early for a lecture I was to give at Sophia University in Tokyo. I decided to kill the time by having an Iced Tea in the school's cafeteria. Simple enough time-killer, right?

Wrong!

So help me, here's how it went: I walked up to the counter. The Japanese man behind the counter asked, "May I help you?"

Now, when a local native says, "May I help you?," I assume that indicates he has a certain knowledge of my native language and desires that we communicate in said language since he was the one who started the conversation in the first place. I mean if he wanted everything to take place in Nihongo, he could have met me mute or said "Hai" or something equally vernacular and I would have given my Japanese a try.

But, no. He instead asked, "May I help you?" in my very own English.

So, I said, "Yes, thank you. I'll have an Iced Tea."

"No," he said.

"No?" I asked.

"No Iced Tea."

Excuse the digression, but I like Iced Tea. And, I like it winter, summer, spring and fall. But back in Cleveland, restaurants begin saying "No" to Iced Tea requests of mine along about the same time the Browns play their first home football game in Municipal Stadium. Because, as far as they are concerned, Iced Tea time is over. When they do, however, I ask, "Do you have hot tea?"

They always answer "Yes."

Then I ask, "Do you have ice?"

And they always say "Yes" to that one, too.

Then I say, "OK, please bring me a cup of hot tea and two glasses of ice." They always get the message and always deliver

20

the Iced Tea. Even on Christmas Eve.

But, back to the Sophia cafeteria. In that case, I decided by the way the counterman said "No" that I'd only get into severe complications with the Cleveland hot-tea-and-two-glasses-of-ice routine. Instead, I just ordered hot tea.

He made it for me, put it in front of me, then said, "Sorry. No lemon."

"That's OK," I assured him. "I'll have milk instead."

"OK," he answered, and immediately dumped the cup of hot tea down the sink next to him and poured me a glass of milk.

Now I hope that at least *you* realize that I meant I wanted milk in the tea instead of the lemon he didn't have. But, he'd already poured the glass of milk and I decided to drink it. But, I still wanted the tea. I tried again. "I want the tea, too."

"Too?" he asked.

At least I thought he asked, "Too?"

But, when he turned around with a pair of cups of tea, I realized that what he really asked was "Two?"

I started to explain to him that communications had totally broken down and that all I really wanted was a single cup of tea with a little milk in the same cup.

But, I decided against it. It was much simpler, I correctly figured — although slightly more expensive — to take the glass of milk and two cups of tea and sit down. And I did.

Just then, the student I met at the door who directed me to the cafeteria in the first place stopped by my table. "I thought you wanted Iced Tea," he remembered.

"I did," I admitted, "but I'm afraid the waiter misunderstood."

"You mean the waiter misunderstood one Iced Tea for two hot teas and milk?" he asked. Then, he advised, "You should have spoken to him in English. They all understand English here.''

Five years ago — back in Cleveland — so did I.

YES, IT *ISN'T* AN EASY LANGUAGE

A fellow registered alien that I met in the Tokyo Hilton lobby the other night told me that she read some of my newspaper articles and that I shouldn't feel bad about my lack of expertise in Nihongo.

''I've been here a lot longer than you,'' she told me, ''And I speak and understand less than you do.'' In fact, she further confessed, her own level of fluency wasn't going up any, either, these days. ''You see, I've been here so long that I don't even dare admit there's anything about the language I don't know,'' she said. ''So, I'll never learn any more than I know now.''

Now I started comforting her. ''Don't be silly. I've heard you speak Japanese. You do fine.''

''At some of it, yes,'' she agreed. ''But what I don't know, contrary to the old adage, does hurt me.''

''How?'' I wanted to know.

''Right now, for instance,'' she said, looking at her watch. ''It's almost nine o'clock and I'm starving.''

''Because of a lack of knowledge of Japanese?'' I asked. ''Ridiculous. Surely you know how to order a meal in Japanese.''

''Of course I do,'' she confirmed. ''But that's not why I'm starving.''

''Then why?''

"Because," she said, "One of the things I've never learned is how to tell time in Japanese. Oh, I can say the right words for exact hours like eight o'clock or nine o'clock or ten o'clock. But I don't know how to say eight-thirty, for instance."

"So?"

"So, tonight I wanted to meet these two Japanese girl friends here for dinner. Their English isn't so good, so when I invited them over the phone, I used my pidgin Japanese."

"And?"

"And, I knew I couldn't get here tonight until a little after eight o'clock. I was going to ask them to be here at eight o'clock. But, they're usually prompt and would have been here at eight on the dot. Then, when I was late, I imagined they'd think they'd misunderstood me about the day or the hotel and they'd go home."

The light dawned on me. "And so, since you couldn't say eight-fifteen or eight-thirty, you had to make it nine o'clock?"

"Exactly," she sighed. "I'm starving."

Just then, her Japanese friends came and they took off like a shot, barely able to keep up with the Gaijin as she raced off toward the restaurant.

I started to feel sorry for her, but I decided she's still better off than a lot of other Gaijins I know — even though they can say eight-thirty in Japanese.

Because, she obviously knows what she doesn't know and works around it. Those others think they understand, and they don't.

Like I have a friend who really thinks Japanese mean "Yes" when they say "Hai." I've tried to tell him a thousand times that, "Hai" from a Japanese means only that he heard a sound. Not "Yes, I understand" or "Yes, I agree" or "Yes, I'll do what you say." Just that he heard the sound.

23

This same friend doesn't even listen when I tell him that "Ah so desu ka" means the same thing as "Hai" — only it takes longer to say — and not "yes", even though the speaker's head may be bobbing up and down as he says it.

Japanese almost never say "No," and if they do, it probably is as close to "yes" in meaning as they'll ever approach. Like if you ask "Aren't you coming?" and, they want to come, they can't answer "Yes." Because, they feel, "Yes" would mean — in answer to such a typically-phrased Gaijin question — "Yes, I'm not coming." But, since they really want to come, they have no alternative but to answer "No" to indicate agreement.

That may sound complicated, but it's not nearly as complicated as "sumimasen." It took me almost two years to find out what that word meant, because the Japanese pronounce it "see-mah-sen" and I couldn't find such a word in my trusty dictionary. Not spelled that way, at least.

But, it's a great word. It allows Gaijins to call waiters, and elderly Nihonjin ladies with shopping bags to run you down on subway and train platforms. It's also great, repeated over and over, to give to policemen who stop you for going through red lights.

Anyway, as I was thinking about all this the other night standing here in the Hilton lobby, I glanced at my watch. It was 9:45. My Japanese friend, whom I asked to meet me there at nine o'clock, still hadn't shown up. He must be coming, I thought, because when I asked him to join me, he clearly said "Yes."

Although, come to think of it, he'd said "Hai."

24

KORE WA TOIRETTO PEIPAA DESU

The more I move around these tight little islands, the more respect I have for the ingenuity the Japanese apply in getting the most possible use out of the little bit of space they have to work with.

Like you don't see any sprawling lawns surrounding their homes. And because they don't waste the space for the lawns themselves, they don't have to waste the space necessary to store lawnmowers or spray cans and chemicals required to fight the crabgrass.

If you've ever taken a ride on a train or subway in Tokyo, you know they don't waste any space there, either.

And weren't the Japanese the ones that figured out how to make radios and calculators so small that they could fit in your wallet?

On the other hand, I never felt the same way about the Japanese when it comes to how they use their time. You know what I mean, I'm sure. Each time I ask them a question that requires merely a simple "Yes" or "No" answer, they seem to use up hours with a reply that never does really equal "Yes" or "No."

If you're a businessman here, you know how long a Japanese meeting can last. And, despite the time invested, how little is really decided at those meetings.

But I read something in the paper last week that's changed my mind completely about all that. And that was the news that a Japanese paper maker has started the manufacture of rolls of toilet paper with English lessons printed on them.

Actually, however, it wasn't so much a desire to help utilize normally unproductive time that led to the language-lessons-on-toilet-paper idea — according to the news story — as it was to roll up bigger sales of this usually daily necessity. Things haven't been the same for toilet paper people, saleswise, since the great hoarding stampede of a few months ago.

Now, with supply ahead of demand, the paper maker had to do something to keep from being wiped out.

The first rolls off the press introduce — again according to the news story — six English words. The company plans to come up with 13 new words each month. "Regular" customers, the manufacturer says, should be able to tear off 800 new English words in the first year. "Irregular" customers — presumably those over 35 in this Serutan-less country — will learn proportionally less.

After reading the story, I was quite anxious to find out which words were chosen for the maiden rolls. I consider this choice critical. After all, I know if the Japanese language school people were putting out such paper for Gaijins, the first four words would be "Kore wa hon desu." What concerned me was the possibility that the English version might start out with "This is a book."

Now think about it for a minute. If a Japanese learning his English from toilet paper sees "This is a book" written on toilet paper, Lord knows what he might think "Book of the Month Club" sends its members. Or what he might do if you lend him one of your books. He might think it's Western style toilet paper and treat it accordingly.

Anyway, I couldn't find any of this new paper in Tokyo to check for myself, so I called the distributor in Yokohama. Either one of the "Irregulars" answered the phone, or he never wears his glasses in the men's room. He didn't know which words were in Book I (or do you call it "Roll I?"), but he did know they were chosen especially for the program by a professor. He assured me that there were basic English words

26

on each roll, and that they were taken from a list of words usually taught in high school level English classes here.

The words, he says, are written in Romaji. There is an explanation of how to pronounce them, and a brief summary of the meaning of each word. The company has no plans at present to hold regular examinations to determine how students are doing. And, there are no plans to produce similar lessons in Japanese for Gaijins.

The only concern for the success of this particular teaching method is the obvious male chauvinist concern that women will probably pick up more new words each month than men. It's also possible that those in Tokyo most in need of English instructions — the taxi drivers — won't get any lessons at all since there are no plans to hang the rolls on any of their favorite telephone poles.

I'm not upset at all that they are not likely to make similar Japanese language rolls for us Gaijins. I'll be happier, in fact — if by this process of elimination — all the Japanese learn English. As long as we understand each other.

If I were one of the famous language schools in town, I'd be upset, however. It would crush me to see my language laboratory move into the lavatory. And think of all the moonlighting, English-teaching, Gaijin wives that will be retired by a four-roll pack.

I'm certainly not one to pooh-pooh a new idea like this. After all, it does represent a means for an end. But, I'm just a little skeptical — with some reason. You see, we trained our Japanese dog on The Japan Times for weeks, and he's *never* spoken one word of English.

IT'S BREAD THERE ISN'T ANY OF

Whenever first-time-ever-in-Japan visiting fireman arrives at Haneda from the Home Office, I exchange a brown envelope of Tokyo survival essentials for the duty free goodies they bring me.

You can guess all by yourself the contents of the duty free package. I'll give you the details of the Tokyo survival kit.

Number one item in there is a pack of 3×5 cards held together by a rubber band. One card has all the telephone numbers they might ever need here — for our office, my house, the American Embassy, and their hotel. The other cards have instructions written in Japanese (by my secretary), and the decoding equivalent in English (by me), for them to give taxi drivers when they want to go to the office, my house, the American Embassy, or back to the hotel.

Number two item is a map of Tokyo where I've marked all those places for which they have phone numbers and taxi cards.

Number three is a simple English-Japanese and Japanese-English dictionary that will hopefully bail them out of any situations not covered by the cards or the map. (I *don't* give them a copy of my book. In fact, they have to *buy* my book, or I won't even meet them at the airport.)

Now one of the recent visiting firemen suggested that I should also include in the kit one of those handy phrase books since he found many situations requiring more than just a word out of the dictionary. "I would have bought one myself," he said, "but there were so many different phrase books in the hotel book store that I was very confused. *You* know something about this language," he mistakenly went on. "Why don't *you* pick out one for me?"

Now most of you know by now that I can get very upset when I think about Japanese language lessons of any kind — be they from a school or from one of those books. Like take the old standard starter phrase, "Kore wa hon desu."

What good is it?

Think about it for a moment. If it's a Japanese you're talking to, you can't very well point to a book and say to *him* "Kore wa hon desu." *He* already *knows* it's a book. If it's a brand new Gaijin you're talking to, he will probably know it's a book, too, but he won't understand the "Kore wa hon desu." If, on the third hand, it's a Gaijin who's been to language school here, he'll not only *know* it's a book, but *he'll* know what you're going to say the minute you point to that book. He may even say it first to show off.

But, despite all this, I decided to honor his request.

So, next morning I went to the bookstore and, believe me, my fireman was right. I counted 12 different phrase books. I decided to leaf through each of them and pick a winner.

First one was "Japanese in 30 Hours." The random page I turned to had the Japanese phrase for "The mistress is inside the wooden doors." I discarded that one because this particular fireman had his wife with him and, if she picked it up, she might misunderstand the reason for his visit.

Next was titled "Essential Japanese." The first phrase I turned to in that one was "I need a dictionary to read an English language newspaper." Now if he had any use for that phrase, the Home Office wouldn't have sent him.

Another was "Japanese Illustrated." I opened it to a phrase that said, "It will take two hours to drive there since it's 100 miles from here." I quickly figured that was entirely too optimistic a book for a newcomer. Kamakura isn't even 25 miles from my house, and during the New Year holidays it took me *five* hours to drive there.

The next one, "Easy Japanese," looked pretty clever because it had questions *and* answers. I say "clever" because phrase books with only questions always annoy me since I never understand the answers I get when I pop the questions.

But the first Q and A in that book I came across was this:

Q—"What isn't there any of?"

A—"It's bread there isn't any of."

Now if he ever asked *that* question or gave *that* answer while I was with him, I'd be embarrassed.

So, I went on to "Colloquial Japanese." That had a great phrase that goes "I am not speaking in English now. I am speaking in Japanese." But, obviously, if whatever Japanese person you directed that line to hadn't understood the rest of your Japanese, he wasn't going to understand that phrase, either.

"Japanese in a Hurry" features a phrase that meant "Deliver this to the Station Hotel." My fireman was staying at the Hilton, so I decided that phrase could only cause trouble.

A Book called "Basic Japanese Grammar" had a phrase meaning "Please give me some tea." I decided that after visiting a few Japanese companies, he would be much more in need of a phrase that meant "Please *don't* give me any more tea." It wasn't there, so I passed it up.

Finally, I settled on a book called "Romanized Japanese in Six Weeks." He wasn't going to be in Tokyo six weeks (it takes visiting firemen only five days to figure out Japan), but what sold me was a phrase meaning "The price is unreasonable. The price is absurd." I knew he'd find use for that one four or five times a day in Tokyo.

My moment of moments came later that morning at breakfast when I handed him the book. Beaming all over, I said, "Kore wa hon desu."

"What the hell does that mean?" he asked.

"Look it up," I answered.

BACK TO JAPANESE LESSONS, DESHO?

Just last night, I pulled out my list of New Year's resolutions for 1975 to see how I was doing now that the first month has gone by.

The results were not really encouraging.

For instance, I've still not registered for any courses in the Japanese language. I mean, I haven't yet registered this year. Lord knows I've been to every language school in town at one time or another over the past four years, but my Japanese still sounds like I arrived in Haneda last Wednesday.

What really aggravates me, of course, is the fact that the kids are so good at it. Son Donald, as an example, always brings home report cards from St. Mary's School in Tokyo with Japanese language marks in the high 90's. His English marks, unfortunately, are in the mid-70's, but you can't have everything. As I'm sure I've told you before, I've used Son Donald as a translator to buy our car and to talk me out of numerous confrontations with the local traffic police. He even orders the soba by telephone.

Son Sean certainly has no Nihongo problems.

During his studies at Waseda University in Tokyo last year, he met and married a Japanese girl who speaks no English. You don't do something like that with the Japanese you learned in Book One at Naganuma.

Daughter Barbara has no problems, either. Even before

she left for her freshman year at the University of Hawaii last fall where she majors in Japanese, she was reading and writing Japanese, in addition to speaking it.

Wife Sarah — while not as fluent as the kids — is good enough at Nihongo to handle anybody who comes to the door as well as she used to field the Avon Lady and the Fuller Brush Man back in Cleveland.

Only father is still at level of "Kore wa hon desu." And I've spent more time and money studying than *anybody* in the family. Oh, I can say, "hai" and "mushy, mushy" and "ah so desu ka." And, I sometimes add "desho" on the end of English sentences. I can even ask people if they're "genki."

Problem is that their answer, in Japanese, might be, "No, my appendix just burst and I'm on the way to the hospital." That wouldn't mean anything to me, unfortunately, so I would probably just lay "ah so desu ka" on them and leave them wondering all the way to surgery what sort of coldhearted Gaijin I am.

Just before Christmas was when I made up my mind that Japanese lessons would again — for the fifth straight year — be on the top of my list of New Year's resolutions. That's because of another one of those near disasters I can trace quite easily to my sukoshi Nihongo capabilities.

This latest one went like this: I had arranged for a year-end party for our company at the American Club in Tokyo. I arrived about 15 minutes before our Japanese employees (they're *all* Japanese) to check things out. Everything looked fine, except that there was no table for the gifts — called "omiyage" in Japanese — that we had bought for everybody.

Not there's nobody at the Tokyo American Club who doesn't understand English, but I decided to show off — and practice for the party — by asking for this "omiyage" table in Japanese.

Well, the poor waiter I asked almost collapsed. "We thought it was only a year-end party," he said.

"It is," I assured him, "but I also have some gifts."

Now, remember please, all this is going on in Nihongo. Anyway, he ran out of the room and came back with three more waiters — each equally terrified. They were pointing to a place over near the window. I told them no; I wanted it by the door.

More terror.

Finally, one of the waiters — using extremely fine judgement — spoke to me in my very own English. "Are these people who will get married employees of your company, Mr. Maloney?" he asked.

"*What* people who are getting married?" I snapped. Now it was *me* in terror.

"The ones you want the table for," he answered.

"I only want a table to hold the gifts I've brought," and I showed him the boxes.

His color returned. "Then you want a table for 'omiyage' then," he said.

"Of course, I do," I assured him. "That's why I asked him for an 'omiyage' table."

"No, Mr. Maloney," he said, "You asked him for an 'omiai' table and 'omiai' is what we call an arrangement for marriage. I think you foreigners call it 'match-making'."

I remembered then that "omiai" was indeed the word I used, not "omiyage." The relieved trio had the proper table set up in 30 seconds. And we all had a good laugh. Their laugh, of course, was better than mine. I wanted to cry.

So, as soon as the party was over, I started my resolution list with Nihongo lessons on top again.

After all, I worried, suppose my own appendix bursts while I'm in Japan. Who could I tell if Wife Sarah or the kids weren't around to translate?

I only know how to tell them I'm "Genki, desho?"

～～～～～～～～～～～～～～～～～～

DON'T JUST SIT THERE

This is the time of year, traditionally, when people all over the world are busy in a desperate effort to keep New Year's Resolutions that, as you read this, are only four days old. If you're like me, you made the usual ones that you've been regularly making — and breaking — for years.

For instance, all those who resolved to quit smoking in 1976, stand up and cough.

See, you're *NOT* alone.

Now, all those standing who have really stuck to that resolution, for at least the past four days, sit down and *STOP* coughing.

See, only a couple. You confirmed tobacco addicts still standing are not alone, either. I, for one, am standing right alongside you — and still coughing.

Really, it breaks my heart to admit it. What with the 50 per cent price raise the Japanese Government put into effect just before Christmas (Merry Christmas to you, too, Japanese Government) that boosted the price of my Seven Stars to nearly the cost, pound for pound, of a bunch of grapes. I was sure I had all the added incentive necessary this New Year's to kick the habit once and for all.

Well, I didn't have one cigarette all during the day on January First. But then I woke up that night, shook off the residue of New Year's Eve partying and re-read my list of fresh 1976 resolutions. This year there were only three. First, to go

34

on a diet — again. Second, to quit smoking — again. Third, to learn the Japanese language — still again.

Then I started thinking. Any fool knows that if you quit smoking, you gain weight. Right? Ask any fatso and he'll confirm that's true. If you can't find one, call me. I'll confirm by telephone. So, what's more important? Do I quit smoking and avoid all the terminal diseases attributed to cigarettes only to eat even more than I do now and chance a whole new set of terminal diseases?

No, I thought, and decided to go back to smoking like I've done every New Year's Day since 1945.

But after I lit up, I got this terrible taste in my mouth. You know how awful cigarettes taste on an empty stomach. And so, I went downstairs and raided the refrigerator. Resolution Number Two bit the kitchen floor only minutes after Number One. The whole situation made me so mad at myself that I lit up another cigarette to calm my nerves and had another piece of leftover chocolate cake.

So all I'm left with this morning is Resolution Number Three — to really learn the Japanese language. And, unlike the smoking and diet disasters, I think I'm going to make the Nihongo thing this time. When I tell you why I have all this new confidence, I'm sure you'll agree it's well-founded.

If you were here in Japan last May, you'll remember that I then wrote about a new toilet paper on the market that was designed to teach the English language to Japanese people in their spare time. That toilet paper — called ''Please English'' — had English words printed on each roll, along with the Japanese equivalent of each. The idea was that Japanese students could just sit there — Western-Style only, of course — and learn six new English words per roll.

Well, it worked. Despite the recession, the Kyotomi Shigyo company — introducers of ''Please English'' — just reported 1975 business was a record breaker. You've probably noticed yourself how more and more Japanese are speaking more and more English. The rolls are even being exported all over the world.

Business has been so good, in fact, that the company introduced, on New Year's Day 1976, an edition of "Please English" especially for Gaijins who want to learn Japanese. Like the earlier Japanese-to-English version, the new English-to-Japanese version has six new words on each roll, repeated over and over. In each four-roll pack, there are a total of 24 new words.

As a starter, there are 13 different rolls altogether with a total of 78 Nihongo words. By the time 1976 is over, and all of the planned roll lessons are ready for sale, you can learn 936 new words — if you *don't* just sit there. One four-roll pack costs only ¥220, and with 24 new words in each of those packs, the cost of Japanese lessons will come down to only ¥9.1666 per word! Can any language school match that? Especially for such private lessons?

And "Please English" is a breath of fresh air, too. None of the old "Kore wa hon desu" stuff. The six words on roll lesson No. 1, for instance, teach you the Japanese words for "daughter," "garden," "student," "frost," "crow" and "lark." After only a few sittings, you should be able to say — in perfect Japanese — "My student daughter sees a crow and a lark on the frost in the garden."

Using any other method I know, a sentence like that is strictly Book Four material — not just a first-roller.

By the way, you can also buy the "Please English" paper by the case — 24 four-roll packs to the case. And, case by case — as they so often say in Japan — your Nihongo should really improve.

Plus, you'll even be helping the ecology while you're learning. That's because all "Please English" rolls are made from recycled paper. From old Japanese language school tuition receipts, I imagine.

Anyway, I used to be quite disgusted with myself in previous years when I so quickly broke my New Year's Resolutions to stick to diets. But, thanks to "Please English," that won't be the situation in 1976. After all, the more I eat this coming year, the more Japanese I'll learn.

Roll by roll.

Case by case.

II. TRAVEL

Once you're settled in Japan, travel becomes a more substantial part of your life than it ever was before. There are those trips back to the Home Office. And there are Home Leave trips. Plus, there are those weekend trips to see what you can see of your temporarily adopted countryside.

And, they are *all* long trips. I've spent as much time travelling the 25 or 30 miles from Tokyo to Kamakura as I've spent flying non-stop from Haneda to San Francisco.

Since it seems like, no matter where you're going, everybody else is going to the same place on the same plane or train, travel in and around or to and from the Orient is truly a broadening experience.

And, chances are, you'll discover how good a sense of humor you have. I'll explain why I say that.

ROW, ROW, ROW YOUR BOAT

Ever since I can remember, I've spent most of my winters — especially the nasty variety that Mother Nature insists on dropping annually on Cleveland — trying to keep warm.

And, I've spent my summers — especially the steaming ones that the same woman sends to New York and Tokyo — trying to get cool.

It's tough, too, to really be happy in the fall — wherever you are — since fall always brings with it a sort of "batten down the hatches" attitude because you know the nastiest season is coming.

But spring — ah, spring! — is another thing altogether. Spring, more than birthdays, seems to confirm the successful survival of another year of battle with both the natural and man-made elements in life.

In New York, spring meant a long car ride up to the Catskills on Sunday, the blooming of the crocus and the rosebuds, and — the one unfortunate byproduct of the season — the first assault on the crabgrass.

In Cleveland, spring meant a long car ride down through the Ohio farm country on Sundays, the blooming of the crocus and the rosebuds, and — because it respects no state borders — the first assault on the crabgrass.

In Tokyo, long rides are no fun (they're only long in time, not distance), and my yard isn't big enough for crocus, rosebuds, or — thank heaven — crabgrass.

So, what sort of way can you welcome spring here? I decided to consult with a neighbor who has welcomed many Edo springs in his day.

"How about taking a boat ride?" he asked.

40

Now that made a great deal of sense to me. Wife Sarah and I have always wanted to take a cruise. When we were first married, we used to talk about going to Nassau or the West Indies or someplace like that for the standard six nights, seven days. But, no money.

Then, as the years went by, we finally saved up the money. But, by that time, the kids had arrived so we didn't have the six nights, seven days to spare. Later still, we finally came up with both the time and the money. Unfortunately, the kids were ready for college then, and we were back exactly where we started. Still, because the neighbor's suggestion sounded so good, I decided that I should give it some serious thought.

"That's a fine idea," I told him. "Maybe we'll find a quick cruise to Guam or Saipan or even Kyushu. It would be wonderful to get away for a few days and just relax. I only hope it isn't too expensive or takes too long."

"Hold on a minute, Maloney-San," the neighbor interrupted. "That's not what I meant at all. Spring isn't something you 'get away' from, and what I'm talking about takes only ¥120 and very little time."

"Now it's your turn to hold on," I said. "Are you trying to tell me you know of a ¥120 spring cruise — or anything else around here for ¥120, for that matter?"

"Of course," he reassured me. "I wasn't advising a cruise to Guam, I was suggesting an hour in one of those rowboats over in the palace moat."

"A rowboat?"

"Yes," he confirmed, "a rowboat. It costs ¥120 an hour to rent one and I can think of no better way in Tokyo to really get in a springtime mood." Son Donald overheard all this and, obviously, really agreed with the neighbor.

"Come on, Dad," he pleaded, "Let's go and try it."

41

Very seldom does Son Donald — or anybody else in my family, for that matter — come up with any request that requires only ¥120 and an hour's time. So, I agreed, and we were off for the palace moat.

The neighbor was absolutely right on all counts. The boat ticket was only ¥120 and I cannot deny the springtime mood that overcame me.

Those palace stone walls rise straight up on both sides of the water, blocking out Tokyo. The grass-covered slopes — there wasn't a single strand of crabgrass anywhere — were definitely greening.

Up where the slopes join the walls, the trees that line the junction were ready to burst their fabled Sakura all over the place at any instant.

Birds in the trees chirped; ducks in the water quacked; and young couples in the other boats laughed. Even though our rowboat was only making about two knots, if that, we were passing the cars and busses stalled in the traffic on the expressway bridge that cuts across one end of the moat.

This is the life, I thought. There was little doubt in my mind that moat rowing certainly beat a drive through the Catskills or the Ohio farmlands. And I was ready to admit that I wouldn't trade it all for a single rosebud — a rosebud that would soon have to be sprayed with something to discourage Japanese beetles, at that.

And I sure didn't miss the crabgrass, either.

Plus, there was one more ingredient that went a long, long way toward making that rowboat ride an absolutely perfect way to usher in spring.

That was the fact that Son Donald did all the rowing.

NO FRILLS

Every time I go back to the United States after a prolonged interval of time in Japan, it takes me a while to get back in step with my former native version of culture.

Before I go any further, I want to advise newcomers that the above-mentioned ''prolonged interval of time in Japan'' can be almost any period, depending on the circumstances. You newcomers will find that, the way things can go here on occasion, it's entirely possible to spend a year in Japan over any weekend.

Now, back to culture readjustment.

The going-home problems I'm thinking about are the perfectly ordinary ones. Like remembering to tip the waiters, realizing that the taxi door will not open automatically, and keeping your hands off the ''Door Close'' button in the elevators. Driving on the right-hand side of the road is worth a mention, too, I suppose. But not to Englishmen.

Eventually, of course, I do readjust. After all, all of those things were once quite normal circumstances for me before I was transplanted to Tokyo. Every now and then, however, I run into something back home that's brand new to me and my inability to cope shows through my adopted inscrutable Oriental facade.

This summer, my seemingly insurmountable problem had to do with, of all things, the airlines in the United States.

Now I say ''of all things'' because I always felt I was the original Traveling Salesman. I've been more involved in my career with marketing than in any other aspect of business. And why not? Any businessman will tell you that no other part of any business organization has near the importance and impact of the marketing arm (anybody, that is, except the controller and the manufacturing manager).

There's only one drawback to such a job. That's — it's always seemed to me, anyhow — the fact that the only way companies feel they can promote a marketing man is to give him more territory to market in. You know, you start off with a postal zone in New York, graduate to maybe a whole Borough, then take over the so-called ''Metropolitan Area'' from which you move — in about this order — to Northeastern Manager, Eastern Regional Manager, and then the whole U.S. Or, if you stumble somewhere along the line, you could wind up in Japan.

Anyway, it was when I moved out of the Metropolitan chair into the Northeastern seat that I first came in contact with airlines. And it's been a regular affair ever since. In fact, although Wife Sarah and I recently celebrated our 28th wedding anniversary, she's quick to tell anybody that we've really only lived as man and wife for 12 years. The other 16, she points out, I've spent on one airplane or the other without her.

Flying around the U.S. used to be a very simple matter. I'd call the airline, make an economy-class reservation (marketing people always fly economy; it's our way of helping the company recover losses sustained by mistakes made in the finance and manufacturing departments), go to the airport, pick up my ticket, and get on the plane. A very simple matter.

But, that's the way it *used* to be. Not any more. Not on my last trip back, anyway.

Leaving Japan on Northwest was quite ordinary — exactly in the old U.S. sequence I just described. But, once I was in New York, I found I had to make a quick business trip to a plant we have in Fort Lauderdale. So, I called the airline, just like in the old days.

You'll soon see that I couldn't possibly relate accurately

44

what happened after that, but — believe me — the conversation went pretty much like this: "This is Don Maloney of Harris calling. I need an economy seat to Ft. Lauderdale."

"Are you leaving between noon Friday and noon Sunday?"

"I don't know. When are your flights?"

"We have them at all hours, every day. But if you leave any time but between noon on Friday and noon Sunday and stay at least seven days, but come back before 14 days, and you don't plan on going for at least seven days from now and pay for your ticket today, we can make your reservation."

"Well, I'm not sure how long . . ."

"I almost forgot, Mr. Maloney, you must also not be traveling during peak holiday times like Christmas and Thanksgiving or Fourth of July or Eddie Rickenbacker's Birthday."

"All I know is that I have to get to Ft. Lauderdale as quickly as possible. Do you have a seat or no?"

"Not economy or 'no frills' we don't. You see, all the people who fulfill all those other conditions I described a minute ago already have all the seats except for first class."

"You mean you went through all that fuss and set up all those conditions to attract people who *never* fly and left us businessmen — the ones who *always* use the airlines and who never know whether or when we're coming or going — to sit up front where it's twice as expensive?"

"Oh, then you know."

"Know what?"

"That 'no frills' to Ft. Lauderdale is only $61 and first class is twice that at $122?"

"No, I didn't know. But, what do I get in first class for the extra $61?"

"Well, 'no frills' people get only a seat and the right to

45

use the toilet as many times as they want when the 'Fasten Seat Belts' sign is off. No drinks, no food, no nothing.''

''And in first class?''

''For the $61 extra, you'll receive two drinks and sort of a snack lunch and, of course, coffee, tea or milk.''

''For *$61?*''

''Are you shocked, Mr. Maloney?''

''Not really. Because that's exactly what I pay for lunch every day in Tokyo anyway.''

THEY ENJOYED HAVING ME

In the early part of January, I made my first back-to-the-home-office-for-a-meeting trip of 1976. The longer you're in Japan, by the way, you'll begin to notice that you make more and more such trips to the home office, and that home office people will make less and less trips to Japan. After home office people have all their cameras and pearls and woodblock prints, they seem to lose interest in traveling West to the East.

Anyway, I flew Northwest this time to Seattle non-stop, thank heaven. Actually, I *always* fly American-owned airlines across the Pacific. Not so much for the dollar drain — although that's a consideration — but because I'll never be sure that foreign airlines translate everything about precise locations of those oxygen masks, life belts, and rubber rafts when they're making their announcements in English.

Usually, I consider those across-the-Pacific trips rather uneventful. It's always the same, it seems — long, long days coming to Tokyo; short, short nights going the other way.

46

This last time was sukoshi different, however, so I thought I'd tell you about it.

For one thing, I didn't buy one of those $2.50 headsets this time. I'd already made home office trips in November and December (see what I mean?), and I knew the music and the comedy would still be the same on all the channels. Airlines, I've paid $2.50 to discover before, change those taped programs about as often as they replace the airsick bags in the seat pocket in front of you. Of course, not renting the headset also meant I wouldn't get to hear the movie, but I didn't care. Usually, the ''X'' rated movies are ''edited for airline use'' anyway and turn out to be only ''G'' movies as a result. Besides, five years in Tokyo — where I watch TV programs with the sound off and make up my own dialogue — have taught me to enjoy sight-only shows.

And, because I didn't buy those earphones this time, I probably never will again. Mainly because the guy next to me did buy them and I want to tell you what went on.

Now I was in 6A (Smoking Section, Window Seat) and he was in 6B (on the aisle). He bought the earphones right off and, I guess, turned to the comedy channel. For the first hour or so, he sat there giggling out loud. His hair was rather long, and you could hardly see his headset. The two guys in 6C and D — who also passed up the $2.50 opportunity — kept looking over and wondering what I was doing to 6B. I decided to put both my hands up on my tray until he changed channels.

But, when he did, things only got worse. He started singing along with Mitch. Of course, with the plugs in his ears, he couldn't hear himself, and so was belting out ''Jingle Bells'' — they still had the Christmas tapes, as I suspected — at the top of his lungs.

My God, I wondered, how often have *I* done that?

Then, the stewardess came by and asked if we preferred

47

meat or fish for dinner. He answered, loud enough for Japanese fishing boats down below to hear, ''Yes.'' She tried again. He yessed again. After one more try, she brought him fish.

''No meat?'' he bellowed and pointed to my Chicken something — or — other sitting on a pile of rice. She smiled and made the switch.

And, I couldn't help but notice that it was the same stewardess-type smile I've seen so many times before when they bring around the coffee. I know that smile all too well, because — years ago — my doctor made me quit regular coffee and said I could drink only no-caffeine coffee or tea. Now I don't mind hot no-caffeine coffee (like Sanka or Decaf), but I like only iced-tea, *not* hot tea. And, when I refuse the coffee and ask for the Sanka or iced tea, I get that same smile-less smile.

Anyway, after dinner and a couple of iced teas, I got up and made a trip to the lavatory. Only one flashed ''vacant'' through that little hole in the door and I jerked it open.

''Vacant'' it wasn't.

A blond girl in slacks — or I should say, I *thought* they were slacks — sitting there doing exactly, I assume, what I'd come to do, although in a slightly different pose. When I saw her — and she saw me — I felt I should say *something* and shut the door, but I couldn't think of a thing to say then any more than I've been able to come up with an appropriate greeting for the little old ladies who are forever coming into the men's rooms in Tokyo when I'm using them. I just slammed the door quickly to stifle the scream which I'm sure was heard clearly by everyone except 6B, who still had his headset on.

I easily managed to avoid her eyes and further embarassment for both of us as she came back down the aisle — they *were* slacks, by the way — to her seat. It was a much tougher job to ignore her at Seattle where we wound up on opposite sides of the baggage delivery carousel.

Anyway, after customs, I changed to a DC-10 flight to Cleveland and I realized for the first time why I really like that plane so much better than the 747.

It's the lavatories again.

Notice next time you're on a 747. When you've finished your reason for the lavatory visit, and push the flush handle, *nothing* happens. Then, as you have your back to the major apparatus in that room, and are washing your hands, the computer or whatever it is that manages that major apparatus finally gets the "flush" message you sent earlier and all hell of gurgling breaks loose. Coming unexpectedly as it does, I'm usually certain that the cabin pressure stewardesses are always warning about has *really* let go this time and I'm waiting for that mask to drop from behind the mirror — or wherever it is in the lavatories.

But, on the DC-10, you push "flush" and it flushes. Right then. *When* you expect it. *Much* easier on the nerves.

Anyway, as we landed in Cleveland, I thought about what I'd seen and heard that day — or days — on that ride from Tokyo. And, I realize that I am just one of the 8,000,000 stories that take place every day in the Naked Jumbos.

The stewardesses, on the other hand, get a chance to see all 8,000,000.

No wonder — for the entertainment value alone — they sound like they really mean it when they end every trip by saying that they "enjoyed having us."

YES, SARAH, THERE IS A NARITA AIRPORT

For the Maloney family, Sunday was usually "Discover Japan" day. After church, we usually caught brunch somewhere Western and then began our weekly Sabbath adventure.

A couple of weeks ago, I got to pick the new horizon and took off out the Shuto Expressway for Chiba.

"Where to today?" Wife Sarah asked.

"To the airport," I answered.

"Oh, Lord. Who's coming in today?"

Actually, I detected just a slight amount of exasperation in her question. And, I must admit, it was somewhat justified. We were grounded on the three previous Sundays in a row because some visiting fireman or other was either coming or going via Haneda. So, I hastened to assure Wife Sarah that nobody was arriving or departing.

"It's just as well," she said looking out the window, "because you're going the wrong way. You should have turned right back there to get to the airport."

"No, Sarah," I assured her, "we're heading for the *new* airport out at Narita and this is the right way."

"When did they open a new airport?"

"They didn't."

"I'll *never* understand you. If nobody is coming in or going out, we shouldn't be going to an airport at all. Much less to one that isn't even opened yet — even if somebody *did* want to come or go."

"This is just sort of a dry run," I told her. "Someday, this new Narita airport *will* be opened and then we'll have to

50

know how to get there. So, we'll check out the route today and be ready."

"When," asked Wife Sarah, "will Narita Airport open?"

I had to admit that I didn't know that. *Nobody* knew.

"Well, when will it be finished?"

"Oh, it's finished."

"Then," in typical female fashion, she asked, "Why don't they just open it?"

"Because," I tried to explain, "they're having some problems with the local people about moving fuel out to the airport and other minor things."

"I don't understand," she said. "When will they solve the problems."

Because I didn't really understand either, I told her so. And, I added that I had no idea when all the problems would be solved.

"Then what makes you think they'll *ever* solve them?" she wanted to know. "And why are we making a practice run to an airport that's finished but might never be opened?"

I decided to plead with Wife Sarah to have faith in the Oriental process. "Look, remember how when we head West from Shinjuku, we go out on the Expressway for a while? And then we have to go down on that damn Koshukaido Highway for a few miles in horribly heavy traffic before we finally get back on the Expressway?"

"Who could forget?"

"And, remember I told you that the Expressway was already built parallel to the crowded highway, but that some problem with local residents made it necessary for us to get off the Expressway and fight through that Koshukaido traffic?"

"I remember. I remember."

"Well," I said, "just as I have faith that someday *those*

51

problems will be solved and the Expressway opened, so do I have faith the other problems will be solved and the airport at Narita will be opened."

"Now don't tell me," Wife Sarah pleaded, "that we have to go over that problem Expressway to get to the problem airport."

I told her to relax, because we were heading in the opposite direction. Her sigh of relief was clearly audible.

"That's the third toll station we went through since we left Roppongi," she counted. "Are you *sure* we're heading for an airport?"

"I can read the signs, you know," I told her.

"Your ability to read Japanese signs has put us in Sushi restaurants when we wanted Yakitori, so don't offer *that* talent as evidence."

Son Donald, speaking out for the first time during all this, backed me up by assuring his mother that the "Narita Airport" signs were in English as well as in Japanese.

Wife Sarah hadn't noticed the signs and expressed amazement that anybody would even put up signs directing you to an airport that doesn't yet exist. Then, "I assume this new airport will cut down the flying time to Cleveland, by about two hours."

"What," I asked, "gives you that idea?"

"Because we must be at least that much closer now than when we left Tokyo."

Fortunately, we arrived at the Narita Airport entrance just at that moment. "Well," I announced, "there it is!"

Wife Sarah looked where I was pointing. "There *what* is?"

"The new airport."

"But that's just a maze of barbed wire and barriers across the road."

"I *told* you it wasn't opened yet," I reminded her.

"Not open and barricaded like that are two different things. Are you sure this is an airport?"

Again, Son Donald (God bless him!) backed me up.

"Well," I asked, "what do you think?"

"To tell you the truth," she said, "I'm thinking three separate and distinct thoughts right at the moment. For one, I'm wondering if we'll have to get a new Alien Registration when and if we get back to Tokyo from here. Two, I'll never, never complain about the trip to Haneda again."

"And third?"

"Third, I can't wait until we get home and somebody asks us where we've been today."

"Why?" I asked.

"Because I can't believe you could explain all this to anybody who will understand it anymore than I did."

<hr>

MAYBE THE PARTY'S OVER

In the years I've been in Japan, there have been countless occasions when I've kicked myself for not having my Instamatic camera in my pocket.

Most of these kicking times were when I saw some sign or other that gave me a real chuckle because of the unfortunate results of an attempt by a Japanese merchant to translate something into English. I try not to laugh at such signs, because I'm continually haunted by how tragic it would certainly be if some Cleveland storekeeper tried to translate his signs into Japanese.

Still, I laugh.

And, I've always pledged, to no avail, that I would constantly be camera-equipped in order to preserve these fractures on film to share with other Gaijins here and abroad who seem to have my type of humor sense.

Like there was this bakery near Toranomon in Tokyo that advertised its wares by printing — in foot-high letters all across a front awning — "BRDEAD."

Or that beautiful one over the urinals in the men's room at Haneda that asks, "Please don't deposit cigarette butt or other foreign things."

You've probably seen for yourself the many signs in a Harajuku supermarket that warn, "No, Pet Allowed."

I'll bet, in Tokyo alone, there are 50 "Beauty Sarons." Maybe more. Certainly, almost as many as there are "Bar Ber Shops."

There's even one fellow in town who will run off as many copies of maps to your house or business cards as you want, and the sign in front of his shop identifies him as a "Plinter."

Maybe my favorite is "Come Rearn Engrish."

But just last week, a new English sign went up on my street — not five yards from my very own front door — that struck not a single funny bone in my entire body. It says, as clearly as I write it here, "Vehicles Illegally Parked Will Be Towed Away."

Now, obviously, such an English-language sign is not aimed at frightening any native Japanese in the neighborhood. It's pointed right at us aliens who already know that the blue-circle-with-the-red-diagonal-slash-through-it means parking is a no-no.

Up to now, however, slashed sign or no, we Gaijins have always been secure in the knowledge that we could park

54

anywhere and hide behind that old reliable "Wakarimasen" if we got caught.

Well, no more. You can hardly "Wakarimasen" a sign plainly lettered in the language we've been hiding behind all these years.

For the first couple of days after I first saw that sign, my panic level was rather low. I thought maybe the Tokyo police were just test-marketing an idea designed to get me personally to stop complaining more friendly signs around town aren't in English. I even toyed with the idea that some of my friends might have put it up as a joke.

But, as I rode around areas of town normally patrolled by Gaijins, I saw more and more of those same signs — word for frightening word.

So, I am ready to assume that — traffic-wise, at least — the party's over. Soon, I'll bet more than just parking regulations show up in English. And what a shame! And what a difference it will make.

For instance, I've seen those signs on corners a thousand times — the ones with white arrows on a blue background. The arrows sometimes point just straight ahead. Other times, they point straight and right or straight and left. Under those signs, there's usually a little sign that says merely "8-20" or "7-9". I was always ready to claim, if caught disobeying, that I thought that meant that the odds of being able to make that turn without getting mashed by an oncoming taxi were only 8 in 20 on some corners or as good as 7 in 9 on others.

Any day now — mark my words — we're going to see "No Left Turn" or "No Right Turn" or simply "No Turns" just as we did in Cleveland. If — or I should say "when" — they put up English "No U Turn" signs, I'll really be lost. Almost every single time I drive around this town, I have to make a U Turn somewhere just to get where I'm going. Back home, anytime I missed a street I wanted, I'd simply go around the block. If you've driven here any length of time at all, you know Japanese blocks somehow *never* go around. A U Turn is the only answer.

Or it was. It won't be for long.

Actually, my problem with traffic signs wasn't spawned in Tokyo. I had the same problem in New York when we lived there.

Take just parking, for instance. New York signs include plain old "No Parking." But sometimes they post "No Parking *Anytime.*"

Did that mean that where there was just "No Parking," without the "Anytime" added, that it was OK to park sometimes? I never got a clear ruling.

Or how about the "No Parking or Standing or Stopping or Discharging Passengers" signs in New York. Is there a difference between "Parking" and "Standing" or "Stopping?" Can you "Stand" and "Stop" all the time in a place that says "No Parking Anytime?" Can you *pick-up* passengers in those places where you can't *discharge* them?

The only New York parking sign I ever really understood was the one that said, "Vehicles Illegally Parked Will Be Towed Away." Unfortunately — like I said — that's exactly what it says on those new Tokyo signs.

Indeed, the party's over.

SEA FOR YOURSELF

While we were back in the United States last summer, at least a dozen people asked what the Ocean Expo thing down in

Okinawa was all about. "I can't understand," each one was saying — more or less, "how anybody can run an international exposition using just the sea as a theme."

Now I didn't want to tell them at the time, but neither could I. So, I had to admit that I hadn't been to Okinawa ever and didn't know anything about Ocean Expo. I'd always felt that I'd seen enough of the sea just flying back and forth across the Pacific between Tokyo and Cleveland. In fact, the only sea I've ever really enjoyed is that portion of it that laps against the beach at Honolulu — and then only when I've been sprawled out on said beach.

Anyway, after we returned from the U.S., Wife Sarah began pushing for a trip to Okinawa. Not because she had any desire to see Ocean Expo, but because she wanted to visit Son Sean who is stationed with the Air Force on Okinawa and living there with his family. And so we went.

Okinawa itself I found quite interesting. For one thing, they drive on the right-hand side of the road there. Oh, they drive the same way they do in Tokyo, but they do it all on the other side. That's interesting.

And along the roads, they have any number of drive-in restaurants. I mean real drive-ins, where you pull up and tell them via microphone what you want on your hamburger and what size root beer you have in mind — just like in Cleveland. There's just one small rub in Okinawa: The girl on the other end of your car-side speaker answers in Japanese. That's not an impossible situation, however, because our "hamburger" and "root beer" is not too far off from her "hambaga" and "looto beeru." "Hold the pickles," however, is a problem. But interesting.

So is the surprise meal she brings you.

Food prices in Okinawa are really cheap. And, they have almost everything. I mean you can buy any kind of meat, even liverwurst. Old Grandad bourbon is available. For peanuts, too. Cheaper even than back in Cleveland. We spent hardly nothing on food and booze in Okinawa. Of course, I should point out that Son Sean bought it all for us in the commissary at the air base. I'm not sure about the prices in the other kind of stores on the island. But, Okinawa is part of Japan, so I'm sure you'll find prices interesting, too. To say the least. Or, I should say, the most.

And we did get to see Ocean Expo. The first thing I learned on our trip to the Expo site was that little islands on your map, like Okinawa, grow into much bigger islands when you go from one end to the other by bus. Especially on a Japanese bus. To give you some idea of what seemed to prolong the trip, imagine that the same size seats as were in our bus were standard equipment on a 747. Then, economy class seating would be 21 across each row.

We did finally get to Expo, however, and with the help of the entire family, I did finally get out of the bus seat. The fact that I hit my head on the bus baggage rack when I stood up only set back our schedule about eight minutes.

Most important part of the whole trip — aside from seeing Son Sean and his family (and the commissary) — was the discovery that they could indeed — and did — make quite an exposition with only the sea as a theme. In fact, I enjoyed our day there more than at any other World's Fair-type thing I've ever seen.

The various countries with pavilions at Ocean Expo did a great job of explaining their relationships with the sea. The United States' set-up there, I think, was the best my country has ever done at such a show. Even the industrial exhibits were interesting and educational. I especially got a kick out of one that depicted how future sea vehicles will be constructed by mechanically reproducing motive power movements used by various animals'that live in and near the sea.

About the only time I had any discomfort at Expo was in the giant aquarium there. I had the distinct feeling that one of the red snappers looking back through the glass wall there knew I had just eaten his uncle for lunch — raw, at that.

One exhibit showed how we would eventually be living in great underwater cities after we are totally successful in destroying our present environment. Son Donald mused that discovering water in the basement under those future conditions would certainly be considerably more alarming than it was in Cleveland every spring.

All very interesting.

Best part of the whole trip is that we didn't even have to turn in our alien registrations when we left Haneda.

By the way, I forgot to mention that they had a big amusement park area there like all Expos do. And I must confess that we didn't visit it; we skipped that area.

After all — after six years in Tokyo, the last thing I need is another amusement park.

NOT WITH A ROAR, BUT A WHIMPER

A news story I saw out of Yokohama a while ago said the recent — or current, depending on how your business is doing these days — recession had a silver lining. It probably should have said "checkered lining," because, the story said, it solved the problem of the "chronic shortage" of taxi drivers in Japan.

The claim was that — strictly because the recession was cutting into some workers' incomes, particularly their overtime — it was necessary for men with shrinking incomes to find extra work. Over 12,000 applied for taxi driver jobs in a time period when usually only 4,000 would apply.

Now I was shocked when I read about that. Not because of hearing about the recession, but because it's the first time I ever heard about any "chronic shortage" of taxi drivers. I was under the clear impression — without actually counting — that just as many taxis were passing me up at night now as passed me up at night two years ago. And there always seems to still be one driver for every telephone pole.

Also, I thought just as many cabs were parked over by Aoyama cemetery in Tokyo these days as there ever were.

See how impressions can mislead?

A very, very interesting part of the news story was a report of a conversation with a taxi company owner. He said that not only was the recession good for solving the driver shortage, but it was doubly good for taxi passengers. That's because new drivers have much "greater courtesy" toward their riders.

I guess when I do finally get a taxi in Tokyo, it's always driven by a seasoned veteran.

One aspect of all this that I wasn't shocked about was the fact that some men would turn to taxi-driving to beef-up their income. I did that myself once when we were living in New York.

It was more than 21 years ago, I'm sure, because I remember that the reason I started hacking was that Son Sean was about to be born. Wife Sarah had been working and had to quit as Sean's due date approached. I suddenly realized how much her income had meant to us. And, as typical of most marriage beginnings, I guess, a fair-size trauma was caused by the realization that we were about to abruptly go from a family of three (Daughter Frances was already almost three years old) with two incomes to a family of four with one income. So, I got behind the taxi wheel on nights and weekends for awhile.

Anyway, reading about the new drivers with the "greater courtesy" reminded me that perhaps I haven't been fair in the past by reporting only my more aggravating experiences with the meter men of Tokyo.

I'll right all that here and now.

You see, I had this Toyota Crown some time back that had a gimmick which automatically locked all four doors on that car when I locked mine at the driver's seat. And they all unlocked when I did, too.

On occasion, unfortunately, they also — those doors — locked when I got out of the car and slammed the door too hard. That unfortunate thing happened more than once. But, I always had the keys in my hand, so no problem.

Well, not *always*.

Once, out in Kamikitazawa — where we made our first home in Japan — it happened with the keys still inside the car. I was doing the grocery shopping in the so-called "downtown Kamikitazawa" area and realized my plight when I returned to the car with my arms full of packages — including an Occidental fortune in round steak which I somehow gave in to for old times' sake in the butcher shop.

I piled the packages on the roof of the car, ran to a nearby red phone, called home, and asked them to hurry "downtown" (about three blocks away) with the extra set of keys. Maid Machiko finally arrived at the scene of my public face-loss (every passing Kamikitazawan was wondering why I was just standing there with packages on the roof and the motor running. I forgot to mention the motor earlier).

Quickly, I grabbed the keys, ignored Maid Machiko's continued questions about why I locked the car with the keys inside, jumped in, and started for home. Because of Kamikitazawa's one-way streets, I had to return home via a rather large circle. A Tokyo taxi was behind me, constantly blowing his horn.

Now this street was really quite narrow. Another coat of paint on either my Crown or the adjacent buildings and I wouldn't have fit. I went slow in case anybody along that street stepped out of his front door.

But, the taxi continued the horn-blowing. Each time his horn went off, my blood pressure went up ten points. It was already at a dangerous peak over the locked-doors embarrassment, and I decided that when I got to the next intersection — where there would be room for me to open my door — I'd get out, go back to that taxi, and punch the horn-blower right in the nose. And he kept blowing until we got to that intersection.

I leaped out and started at him. He was smiling, and with his arm out the window, was pointing to the roof of his cab over his head. That action startled me, and I looked at the roof of my car.

There was my bag of round steak — and all the other groceries — right where I'd put them earlier so I could get at the phone.

What little face I had left turned quite red. I took the packages off the roof and put them in the back seat. It seemed like it took two hours.

And that's the way it all ended. Not with a punch in the nose, but with a very deep bow.

To, of all people, a Tokyo taxi driver.

III. HOME LIFE

You sometimes find it hard to believe while you're living in Japan, but life *does* go on.

What I'm trying to say is that all of the problems you normally faced in your rather normal home life back in Cleveland — or wherever — continue to crop up. All the new problems you face in Japan are extras — they don't replace the old ones you were used to.

But, thanks to Japan, as normal as those old problems used to appear, they take on a whole new dimension that makes them more interesting than ever.

Like have you ever planned a wedding 10,000 miles from the church? Or tried a diet without knowing how many calories are in bean paste, soba noodles, or any of the other household staples?

You don't have to do either. I'll tell you what happened, when we did.

COCKROACHES — THERE, I SAID IT

One thing nice about living in Tokyo — or *one* of the nice things, I should say — is that it's OK to talk openly about Cockroaches. Not only OK to *talk* about them, but even OK to admit that you have them in your house or apartment.

I say it's a nice thing, because back home we weren't even allowed to *mention* Cockroaches. My mother was convinced that people who had Cockroaches in their houses were bad, bad housekeepers. I remember that there was one kid on our block back in Teaueck, New Jersey, that I wasn't even allowed to play with because my mother spotted a Cockroach once in the dining room when she was over there for coffee one afternoon.

Of course, I grew up believing all those bad stories about people who had Cockroaches. We never had them. At least, I never saw one and my mother never mentioned them. Wife Sarah's attitude I sized up as about the same as my mother's. She lined all our food cabinets with some magic anti-Cockroach paper and had some guy come in and spray everywhere now and then. All that — plus daily scrubbing all around — and, sure enough, I never saw a Cockroach in Cleveland.

Ants, we had. Sometimes thousands and thousands of ants. Wife Sarah never liked the ants and did everything short of burning our house down to get rid of them. But, she didn't look on the ants as a personal reflection of her effectiveness as a housekeeper. I swear I remember her saying — during more than one of the annual ant assaults: "Thank God they're ants and not Cockroaches."

Personally, I never had a Cockroach hang-up. I mean I always pegged Cockroaches as one of the cleanest animals in the world. That's because the only ones I'd ever seen were either in the sink or the bathtub. That, of course, was while I was in the Army or in some hotel someplace — *never* at Mother's or Wife Sarah's house.

Then, we moved to Tokyo.

One night, out in our Kamikitazawa house, I spotted this rather large bug near the downstairs bathroom. He — or it — was pretty fast, but I nailed him — or it — with my shoe just as he — or it — tried to get under the hallway closet door. Now Wife Sarah was no less of a scrubber in Kamikitazawa than she was in Cleveland. So, despite the substantial evidence from the appearance of this brown plastic animal (at least it *sounded* like plastic breaking when I bashed it with my shoe), I decided it must be what we used to call a "June Bug." I flushed the flattened remains down the john and decided not to mention the incident.

During those first few months out there, I bagged quite a few "June Bugs." Some, however, were rather small. And — since they were always around that downstairs bathroom — I decided they were some kind of water bug. (Neither my mother nor Wife Sarah cared about water bugs any more than they cared about ants.)

One day, I decided I *had* to know whether my hallway intruders were June or Water Bugs, and I looked them both up in Son Donald's encyclopedia. Far as I could tell from that, they were neither. Just on a hunch, I looked up "Cockroach." And there it was, sketch and all. There was no doubt in my mind that both our June *and* our Water Bugs were Cockroaches.

Now what, I thought. Do I dare tell Wife Sarah? Could she take one more portion of cultural shock? How many kids aren't playing with Son Donald, I wondered, because their mothers have known all along our June and Water Bugs were Cockroaches?

Finally, I decided to blurt out to Wife Sarah what I knew.

67

With identifiable tears in both corners of each eye, she told me she had known for months, but had kept the secret so I wouldn't think less of her household efforts.

She owned-up that the first one she'd seen months before was one that Daughter Frances' cat was playing with. She thought then that the cat dragged it in from outside. But later she spotted them inside quite regularly while the cat was still outside.

Wife Sarah confessed that she'd bought those little cardboard houses with the sticky bottoms that are designed to trap Cockroaches. But, without her saying, it was obvious that she was afraid the neighbors would see the sticky houses and figure out that we had Cockroaches.

So, she hid them so well that they did no good. Even the Cockroaches couldn't find them.

But, one night we were visiting neighbors. The wife served up a bowl of special snack things she said her husband always brings back from his home office visits. I didn't want to take a treasure like that and said I'd pass.

"Go ahead," she laughed, "help us eat them before the Cockroaches do."

My God, I thought, here's a woman apparently near normal in every other way — but she announces *publicly* that she has Cockroaches!

Unbelieving, Wife Sarah gasped, "You have *Cockroaches?*"

"Sure," our hostess answered, *"everybody* around here does. Don't *you?"*

I decided to salvage some self-respect and quickly answered, "There are some kind of Cockroach-type bugs at our place — they were there when we moved in."

She assured Wife Sarah and I that they'd be there when we moved out, too. And that they were really here even before the

Japanese came to these islands from mainland Asia. We talked about what sprays work best, which sticky houses do the job, why you shouldn't mash them while they're crawling up the wallpaper, etc., etc.

Later, on the way home, I told Wife Sarah how relieved I felt. How it was so great to be able to let other people know you had Cockroaches and to *talk* out loud about Cockroaches.

"Here OK," Wife Sarah said, "But when we go back home on leave, don't you *dare* say a word to my mother."

▩▩▩▩▩▩▩▩▩▩▩▩▩▩▩▩▩▩▩▩▩▩

YOU DON'T KNOW ME . . .

Unless you're fresh off a Jumbo at Haneda and still awaiting your unaccompanied goods, it most certainly has happened to you. If not, it will someday.

Usually, it comes at the most inopportune time possible. Like when your latest home office visitor has returned to Cleveland or, when you've had three straight days at the office without a meeting.

Or, worse than that, it comes while the home office visitors are *still* in town and you're having three no-decisions-reached meetings a day.

The first jolt is always by telephone. And the call always comes *very* early in the morning or *very* late at night. In other words, *no* chance of your missing it. You pick up the phone — after the usual short prayer that the caller speaks English — and the voice says: "You don't know me . . ."

I digress for a minute, but I want to underline that these calls always, e-v-e-r-y time start with that same "You don't know me . . ."

69

Anyway, following that opener, comes: ". . . , but I'm an old friend of Harry Dombrawski in Cleveland. Harry gave me your number and told me to be sure and call you when we got to Tokyo."

Right here, there's usually a short pause in these types of conversations. Mainly because it always takes a while to figure out who Harry Dombrawski is. Realizing the verbal void, you usually recover with a "How is old Harry these days?"

And, they usually answer something like, "Oh, he's working hard like always. Just because his brother-in-law is on your company's board of directors doesn't mean Harry doesn't have to work."

Oh, you realize. *That* Harry Dombrawski.

You recover again. This time with a "Well, good you called. What can I do for you?"

Hoping, of course, that the answer is "Nothing. Just wanted to say hello for Harry and find out where we can leave these six bottles of duty-free Old Grandad Harry paid for and asked us to pick up for you."

But, it's *never* like that. Instead: "Harry said you know Tokyo and can take me and the wife on a first-class tour — much better than JTB."

Thinking more of the brother-in-law than Harry, you say, "Sure, when are you free? And what would you like to see?"

"Well, first we'd like to see the fish market at Tsukiji. Harry says it's nothing, though, unless you get there around 5 a.m., when all the action is on. And, we want to go tomorrow because Harry said we should go the first morning. He said that on account of the time change, we'd be up at four in the morning, anyway. How about picking us up at the Hilton in the morning about 4:30?"

"OK" — in my case, I manage to get it out *without* crying — "4:30 a.m. at the Hilton."

"Gee, Dan, that's great. Hope your lovely wife, Sally, will be with you."

I decide not to tell him that I'm Don, not Dan. Nor that Wife Sarah is Sarah and not Sally. I just say: "No, afraid not. She's allergic to fish." Actually, Wife Sarah is really allergic to a.m. of any hour and wouldn't be there at 4:30 if it was Betty Ford that was calling.

"Too bad. Well, maybe she can join us after the fish market when you take us over to buy the pearls. Harry says they're dirt cheap in Tokyo."

That isn't really time to tell him that *dirt* in Tokyo — if it's in the right spot — goes for ¥11 million a tsubo. Besides, every time I do that, they ask me what a "tsubo" is and I still don't know, except that it's bigger than a bread box and smaller than an acre. So, instead, "Maybe she will."

"Certainly she will, after lunch when we go for the cameras. That reminds me, don't make any plans for lunch, Dan. We want to buy your lunch at the American Club. Harry says it's great."

I start thinking of tomorrow's meeting schedule. Plus the fact that they can't pay at the American Club and wondering if Harry tipped them off to that, too. "Do we," I ask, "have to do the fish, the cameras, the pearls *and* lunch all tomorrow?"

"Oh, sure," he says. "We have to do it all tomorrow so that Wednesday and Thursday will be free time."

"Free time?"

"Yes, free time. So you and Sally can show us the town. You know the shrines, Mt. Fuji, Palace Gardens, Tokyo Tower, Nikko — you know."

Oh, how I know! How come, I wonder, has he missed the Ginza and the Oriental Bazaar?

He didn't.

"And, of course," he goes on, "to the Ginza and

71

Oriental Bazaar. But first, tomorrow at 4:30. Goodnight.''

I put down the phone and turn to Wife Sarah. "Remember Harry Dombrawski?"

"*Remember* Harry Dombrawski? How could I forget? Don't you remember that he came with his wife a couple of years ago when you were all tied up at the office, and I wound up taking them to buy pearls, cameras, and over to the Ginza, Oriental Bazaar, Meiji Shrine, Tokyo Tower, the Palace Gardens, Nikko and Mt. Fuji?"

"Oh, yeah," I admit. "I remember. Well, listen, that phone call just now. Tomorrow, how about . . .''

"Hold it," Wife Sarah cut me off. "My plans for tomorrow — and for Wednesday and Thursday are already made.''

"But, Sarah, I'm all tied up at the office and I really need you to . . .''

Another cut off. This time, "Look. I'd rather do most anything for you than what I'm committed for during the next three days.''

"What," I asked, "is that?"

"After you left for work this morning this old schoolteacher friend of your brother's called.''

"And?"

"And she's in Tokyo on a tour and I'm taking her — and her schoolteacher friend — to the Ginza, Oriental Bazaar, the Palace Gardens, Tokyo Tower, Meiji Shrine, Nikko and Mt. Fuji.''

"A friend of my brother's?"

"You," Wife Sarah assured me, "don't know her."

72

HANDS OFF

Maybe it's just a sign of my arrival at advanced middle age as Wife Sarah so often suggests, but, lately, I oppose rather strongly things labeled as "progress." More and more, I'm for the status quo. With a vengeance.

It wasn't always that way with me, but it sure is these days.

For instance, I remember how glad I was to hear — as a more than somewhat regular air traveler — that the Jumbo Jets were coming. That soon we'd all be flying around in planes that were four times the size of the ones we used to tremble in.

Then, the Jumbos did, indeed, arrive. And, they were, indeed, four times the size of their predecessors. But, once inside a Jumbo, I realized that there were *five* times as many people in the *four* times size. And, worse than that, Jumbos brought decisions, decisions, decisions.

Like in the old days, the only thing I had to decide in seat selection was whether I wanted an aisle or window seat. Simple. (The company already made the economy or first class decision for me.)

Now, I have to decide whether I want a window seat, an outside aisle seat, an inside aisle seat, an inside no-window or no-aisle seat, smoking or no smoking seat, and watch-the-movie or don't-watch-the movie seat. (The company continues to spare me that other decision.)

Progress? Maybe for people who like to sit four-abreast while their palms sweat.

Then, there's the pocket calculator. You know, the one that you just turn on, push the buttons, and watch the answer to your add, multiply, divide, subtract problem shine right out for you.

73

I embraced that promise of progress for a while, too. I think I'm on my third or fourth calculator now. But, the price is high.

Wife Sarah no longer balances her own checkbook because, she says, her batteries are dead. Son Donald doesn't know two times two if I don't lend him my machine. And his math marks at St. Mary's attest to the fact I hate to lend it to him.

I used to be able to divide any price in the Oriental Bazaar by 300 in my head to find out how much that very, very old hibachi was in *real* money. Now, if I don't have that calculator, I have trouble dividing by three. Worse than that, it turns out I never *did* care what the square root of 117 was.

But, right at the moment, I'm a real victim of the latest rage of progress — the digital watch. And, saddest part of it all, I have nobody to thank but myself.

You see, right before Christmas, when Wife Sarah wanted to know what I was looking for in the way of presents, I told her only one thing appealed to me at the moment — a genuine Seiko Quartz Liquid Crystal Digital Watch.

And, obedient wife that she is, that's *exactly* what I got.

Now for about twenty nine minutes, I was thrilled to tears with my new timepiece. Just one glance at my wrist, I could tell it was 4: 38, that it was PM, and that the date was the 28th. By pushing the stem in, a new set of numbers showed in all the windows and now, by pushing a couple of other buttons below the watch face, I could use it as a stopwatch measuring tenths of seconds, seconds, and minutes (up to 60). Pushing one more button stops everything and a sign that says "Lap" lights up while everything else is still timing away underneath to continue to figure the total time while I'm reading the lap time. I can get back to that total time by pushing another button. One more button even lights up all this at night.

74

Like I said, it was great fun for awhile. For example, I determined — thanks to the buttons — that it took our plane 36.8 seconds to take off for a post-Christmas visit to Cleveland. It took, I discovered, 26 minutes, 12 and seven-tenths seconds to drive from our Cleveland hotel to the home office. One minute commercials on Cleveland TV last only 50 seconds. Just tons of information I couldn't have done without.

But, trying to decide merely what time it is presents some problems. Oh, it clearly says 2:36 when it's 2:36, but exactly how much time that gives me to get to the bank before it closes, I don't know. With the old dial, maybe I couldn't see *exactly* what time it was, but I'd know *exactly* how long I had to get to the bank.

In my new quartz, liquid crystal, digital life, ten minutes to two is gone forever. Now, it's one fifty one. But, how long is that before two? Who knows? And rarely before did I not know my PM from my AM without the digital display. Now, I even waste four tenths of a second checking *that*.

The only fun the new watch ever gives me is when I upset another digital owner. Try this yourself on your friends. You see, everyone buys a digital because of the promise of absolute accuracy — only one-sixth of a second gain or loss in a year.

So, when you see a friend with a digital watch — and your watch is telling you quite accurately that it's 4:38 — lie a little and say, "Well, it's 4:53 and I have to go." As your friend hears you say "4:53" he won't be able to resist looking at his watch — which will, of course, show the correct 4:38. Then, watch him shake his watch, tap it, bang it on the table, etc., as you walk off into the night. Works every time.

I'd like to tell you more about all this, but Wife Sarah wants to go over to Akihabara and look at microwave ovens that she says can cook turkeys in four minutes and 30 seconds.

I'm going to check it out, and if it takes one tenth of a

75

second longer by my digital watch, we're sending it back.

And seeing as where we're going is next door to where she got the watch, that's going back, too.

Just as sure as my old watch's big hand is on ten and the little hand is on two.

SMOKING IS A DRAG

Before I sat down to write this, I was desperately trying to remember when I smoked my first cigarette. Not the exact day, but about how old I was. I'm not sure, but I think it was while I was in the seventh grade — so I must have been about 13 or 14.

I *do* remember distinctly, however, the circumstances. A friend of mine back in Teaneck, N.J. had this great toy — a little steam shovel. While you had to make it work by hand, it did have a boiler-like part in the back where you could build a real fire.

He used to go out behind his garage after school — after first announcing his plans to his mother and asking permission to light the fire — to play with the steam shovel. Actually, the steam shovel, and the fire in it, was only a cover in case somebody — especially his mother — noticed smoke rising over the garage. Because, my friend had *no* intention of playing with the steam shovel; he was sneaking his daily after-school cigarette. Wings, I remember, was the brand name.

Simon-pure that I was, I only played with the steam shovel while he smoked. For the first few months, anyway. Then one day, after turning down countless previous offers, I took my first drag. My chest heaved, my eyes watered, and I coughed

76

until I thought I'd lose my tonsils. Without so much as a second drag. I swore off smoking for life.

But the next day, my friend convinced me to give it a second chance. I did. The chest heave was calmer, hardly no tears came to my eyes, and I stopped coughing after the third or fourth drag.

I was hooked.

Expenses, however, went way up. The Wings cigarettes then cost 10 cents a pack. So did the Sen-Sen I had to buy to disguise my nicotine breath before I went home.

That expenditure meant I had to give up my ice-cream cones after school and the Saturday matinees at the movies. By the second Saturday, I realized there was no hope of my living without seeing the next chapter of Flash Gordon, so I swore off the cigarettes again. After all, I couldn't very well ask for a raise in my allowance. My mother would surely have asked why.

A few years later, in high school, I started up my smoking again. It was mandatory to smoke in my high school. The kids who didn't weren't trusted by any of the others with anything. Except, perhaps, for standing guard inside the Boys' Room door in case a teacher came in.

I hated that Boys' Room cigarette-sneaking I remember, because you were very likely to catch pneumonia. You see, there was no such thing as a steam shovel cover there for the smoke, so the windows were always wide open. Teaneck winters got quite cold.

Still, I smoked.

While I was in the Army, my consumption went up to two packs a day. I didn't care — the PX price was right. But, increased cigarette consumption brought on some increased chest consumption, too, so I swore off again.

Needless to say, the cough soon went away and the

cigarettes soon came back. And in no time, I was back to the two-pack-a-day thing.

Just before I came to Japan, I quit smoking for about two years. I bragged to everybody how easy it was to quit. "Are you the master or is tobacco the master?" I asked the weaklings. I even started to show them how I could take a puff of their cigarettes anytime I wanted and still stay pure.

Well, I *did* take a puff anytime I wanted. But, I *didn't* stay pure. Back to the daily two packs.

Once here in Japan, I decided that I couldn't afford my old favorite American cigarettes any longer. And, I certainly could never smoke those terrible Japanese kind.

Wrong again. Half-wrong, anyway.

I certainly could not afford American cigarettes here. Not at ¥360 to a dollar, and absolutely not at ¥290 to a dollar. So, I swore off again. From American cigarettes.

Now, I still have the two-pack-a-day habit, but it's Seven Stars — one of those "terrible Japanese kind." I've never had any trouble quitting cigarettes here, because I've never tried.

Back in Cleveland or New York or Teaneck, cigarettes were forever going up in price by two cents or three cents a pack at a time. Each time, I swore I'd quit. But, what's two or three cents? That was a cheap price to pay for having no will power.

But, I'm sure you know by now that while prices go up in Japan just as often — or oftener — than they do in Cleveland or New York or Teaneck, the Japanese don't fool around with two or three yen at a time. When they raise prices, they *raise* prices.

And soon, joining with already raised taxi fares, bus fares, gas and electric bills, road tolls and all the rest, cigarettes get their turn. To the tune of an average 48 per cent increase per pack.

Now I'm first to admit that my pledges to go on a diet never were honored. And, I've never really stayed with a promise to stop smoking, either. But, my incentive to quit the cigarettes is about to go up 48 per cent. And so, when the price goes up, I'm going to smoke my last Seven Star.

The way I figure it, during the next 12 months that will save me about ¥109,500. Son Donald turned 14 the other day, so I know one thing I won't do with part of those savings is buy him a toy steam shovel.

2.2 POUNDS PER KILO

Some of you, I know, remember that I announced here a few months ago that I was going on a diet. And, you'll recall that I pledged to stick with the diet no matter what. I was determined to get rid of the flab that makes me look like a disguised Gaijin Sumo wrestler — the flab that I've carried since long before I ever heard of Takamiyama.

And, I was determined. As determined as I'd been when launching any of the previous 937 diets I'd started since the fourth grade back in Teaneck, New Jersey, the first time another kid called me ''Porky.''

Those other 937 diets that failed, I decided, failed because they were private diets and nobody knew but me when I rolled off the calorie wagon.

So I decided to make that last diet public — right here where everybody could read about it. That way, I reasoned, it would be a matter of honor — or, more appropriately under the current Oriental circumstances, a matter of face — if everybody knew what I was promising.

79

Friends and foes alike, I thought, would then speak out when they caught me cheating and so force me to follow the rules.

Well, it didn't work.

Oh, not that people didn't say something when they caught me with a two-scooper at Baskin-Robbins. And not that they didn't shake a finger or two at me if they happened on me making a third or fourth trip to one of the Sunday buffet tables at the Tokyo American Club.

You all, in fact, did your part as expected. You normally skinny people did, anyway. My overweight acquaintances, coming off 937 diet failures of their own, merely gave me a relieved smile when they noticed gluttony winning my war.

But, all that didn't help one carbohydrate. It just drove me underground. I learned to park a block away from Baskin-Robbins and send Son Donald out for my two-scoopers.

And I switched to buffets in hotels that only unrecognizable tourists knew about. And kept candy bars in the glove compartment of my car.

Why, I even stopped off for a Big Mac and Chocolate Shake on the way home so that Wife Sarah would be pleased at how little I ate for dinner.

Of course, I was disappointed with my failure to shed any of the girth that is of some advantage only when you're flying (airlines still weigh only the luggage to figure excess baggage charges; *not* the passenger and luggage together).

About the only bright spot in diet failure number 938, I thought, was that I hadn't — at least — gained any additional flab.

I knew that to be true because I arrived in Tokyo weighing 257 pounds — and I got on my Japanese scale every morning and saw the dial needle to 117 kilos. Multiply it yourself; that's 257 pounds. Never changed an ounce — or is it a gram? —

since the day I arrived.

That scale, in fact, was one of the first things I bought when I arrived here. Actually, it only really goes up to 100 kilos on the dial. I couldn't find any that went up as high as the 117 I needed. But, a salesman in Takashimaya pointed out that his scale dial started around a second time after it got to 100, and proved it by having me step on. And he was right. It passed 100 and stopped at 17 kilos and the second pass. See, he said, 100 plus 17 is 117. I bought it. And checked every day. Always, 117 on the nose.

But — and this is what hurts — chores on my recent trip to the U.S. included a medical exam. The Cleveland doctor's scale registered — hell, it *screamed* — 266 pounds!

Impossible, I screamed back.

Not only possible, the doctor suggested, but positive. I'd gained nine pounds. That's what he and his silly non-kilo scale said, anyway.

When we came back to Tokyo, I went right from Haneda (no excess baggage charges on the flight over) to our bathroom scale. It read 117 kilos on the nose. Relieved, I told Wife Sarah the story of the Cleveland scale for the first time.

"See," I said, "I was right. No gain at all. I'd had to have gained as much weight as that flight bag of yours," I told her "to be up to 266." Then, I told her to hand me the flight bag while I was still on the trusted scale to see how close my guess was.

The dial needle didn't move when she handed me the bag. It stayed right at 100 kilos plus 17. Panic-stricken, I grabbed my jumbo suitcase and reboarded the scale. Still 100 plus 17.

"Maybe," Wife Sarah pointed out (knowing damned well she meant "definitely") that, "the scale only goes as far as 17 on the second time around."

Well, that did it.

Diet number 939 was born at that instant. And I won't rest until that needle quits under 100 on the very first pass.

Goodbye forever to two-scoopers — in person or delivered a block away — and to buffets — on familiar or on strange ground. And only flashlights, maps and accident report forms will be in my glove compartment.

This time, I'm serious.

It's a matter of face.

And, of double chins, a fat belly, and a broad rear end under that face.

<hr>

ICED TEA—ON THE ROCKS

Surely I mentioned before the fact that I prefer to drink Iced Tea more than any other liquid concoction I can think of. I mean I *like* Iced Tea. And I like it weak, with just enough liquid artificial sweetener to equal about three spoons of sugar (no calories that way — and, besides, sugar *never* seems to dissolve in Iced Tea), and a good squeeze of juice from about one-quarter of an average lemon.

And not just during the steamy afternoon of summer, either. I like my Iced Tea every hour of every day in every season. But, being such a dedicated Iced Tea person is not without problems.

For one thing, I like a big glass of Iced Tea as soon as I hit the office every morning. I'm sure the girls would be much happier if I'd take the green, warm, local variety like everyone else. But, I find green tea a trying experience in the afternoon, a difficult experience in the evening, and impossible to face in the morning.

82

So, I start my day with a glass of Iced Tea on my desk, the refills keep coming, and I end the day the same way.

That brings me to the first of the Iced Tea problems. Especially when I used liquid sweetener and bottled lemon juice like I do in the office. Because, that formula creates just a glassful of amber liquid — with ice, of course. The absence of the remains of a squeezed lemon makes the drink look very much like a heavy bourbon and water sitting there.

I never realized that it looked quite like that until one day, while we were negotiating a license agreement with one of Japanese partners, I asked their representatives if they'd like to just once to skip the green tea we usually served them and try some of the Iced Tea that I always drink.

"Iced Tea?" all three of them chorused. "That stuff you always drink is *Iced Tea?*"

I assured them it was, indeed, and they all went into a fit of laughter. It seems that for weeks they thought they were doing business with a real two-fisted boozer from Cleveland and seriously wondered whether I was ever sober enough to conclude a binding agreement.

A similar situation came up once back in Cleveland right after we moved there from New York. The street we moved to housed a group of neighbors who loved outdoor barbeques. The job of host rotated from one house to another and the first one we attended was the one held right in our own backyard.

While the roast beef was turning on the spit (you remember roast beef), I served the Gin and Tonics, Martinis and Manhattans on the Rocks, and the Scotch and Waters. All during this, of course, I stuck to my Iced Tea — replenished every once in a while by ducking into the house and filling my glass from a jug kept in the refrigerator. That day was a scorcher, and I must have downed a full gallon or more of Iced Tea. Next barbeque outing was at the house across the street.

83

The host asked me what I wanted to drink and I told him, "Iced Tea."

"*Iced Tea?*" he gasped.

"Iced Tea," I repeated. "I drink *only* Iced Tea."

"You're not serious," he smiled.

I assured him I was and he roared with laughter. "Wait till I tell the rest of the neighbors. All they've talked about since the barbeque at your house is how incredibly well you hold your liquor. They were sure you were drinking Scotch or Bourbon all afternoon. Wait till I tell them!"

Well, he *did* tell them, and they finally became believers.

For awhile, anyway.

You see, there's another problem connected with Iced Tea drinking — particularly when you order Iced Tea when everybody else is ordering booze. And that's the fact that everybody decides you must be an alcoholic and *that's* why you're Iced Teaing it.

So, just to kill that idea, I have a Bourbon Manhattan every once in a while. And, one night back in Cleveland right after all the neighbors bought the Iced Tea story, I stopped in a bar with some of the boys from the office. It turned out to be a rather prolonged Bourbon Manhattan evening. I didn't realize exactly *how* prolonged until I got off the stool to drive home. It was an exciting ride.

When I pulled up in our driveway, I was determined that Wife Sarah wouldn't discover what I'd been up to. So, I chewed all five sticks of Dentyne and walked into the house ever so slowly and carefully. I held my breath while I kissed her hello — on the cheek — and backed away. I was sure she didn't notice my problem.

"You're late, you know," she said, "and we have a dinner appointment with the neighbors up the street. Don't take off your coat; let's go."

I had forgotten about the dinner and did my best to walk a straight line across the street to the neighbors' place. Wife Sarah still wasn't on to my condition, I was convinced.

We walked into the neighbors' living room. Everybody on the street was already there and they all seemed to be staring right at me. Wife Sarah grabbed the lapel of my jacket with one hand, pointed to my reddened face, and redder eyes, with the other hand and announced, "Iced Tea!"

They all laughed. And laughed and laughed. They were still laughing when I collapsed. I missed dinner, but swallowed all the Dentyne Gum.

And, I went back to Iced Tea.

JUST ONCE I'D LIKE TO SEE...

Some time ago, I told you about a parlor game that was sweeping through the Gaijin ghettos of Tokyo. Informally, the game was called "You've Been in Japan Too Long."

If you were here back then, and remember the game I'm talking about, then maybe "You've Been in Japan Too Long" yourself. In case you weren't, however, it went something like this: Depending on your voiced reactions to various daily Japanese incidents, others playing the game decide whether or not you qualify.

For example, if it no longer bothers you when the guy at the other table in your favorite restaurant slurps his soup or picks his teeth then "You've Been in . . . etc." The same holds true if you remember which pocket you put your ticket in when the train ride is over, or if you begin lots of otherwise English-language sentences with "Ano ne" and end them with "desho."

Likewise, if you smoke Hi-Lites or Seven Stars.

Anyway, what I want to tell you about today is a new parlor game that you can hardly avoid these days on the Gaijin circuit in Tokyo. Again, no formal name has been given to the game, but you can recognize it by the fact that each player starts his turn by saying "Just once I'd like to see . . ." and then adds on to that something like "A Tokyo taxi driver beg me to get into his cab at 11:30 some night at Roppongi crossing."

Next player — usually the one to his right (or left, if *you've* been here too long) — now has to come up with what the group considers a better "Just once I'd like to see . . ."

Chances are you haven't yet been exposed to the new game — especially if you're a Real-Japan-Out-Of-Tokyo type. So, because I don't want you to be taken by any visiting big city slickers who may invite you to play sometime soon, I'll give you a short run-down on some of the "Just once I'd like to see . . ." finishers that were good enough to enter some recent games here.

One game I watched last Saturday night — I didn't play — went like this: Player One: "Just once I'd like to see some businessman here whose wife wasn't teaching English on the side."

(I digress for a moment here, but the player who starts the game is decided on the basis of who has been in Japan the longest. This is the only connection I see to the other game I mentioned. Now back to the sample game.)

Player Two: "Just once I'd like to see some businessman whose wife wasn't taking Ikebana lessons *while* she was teaching English on the side."

Player Three: "Just once I'd like to see Takamiyama — Jesse — in a navy blue suit with a white shirt and striped tie."

Player Four: "Just once I'd like to see the day when I need help carrying ¥30,000 worth of groceries out of Kinokuniya."

Player Five: "Just once I'd like to see a little kid on the subway get up to give his seat to some old lady with crutches instead of vice-versa."

Player One (there were only five players in this particular game): "Just once I'd like to see a seat on the subway."

Player Two: "Just once I'd like to see the face of a sushi shop owner if somebody asks him to deep fry the raw mackerel."

Player Three: "Just once I'd like to see the guy with enough guts to solve all his home office visitors' problems by taking them out for a 'fugu' liver dinner."

Player Four: "Just once I'd like to see a hostess in Ginza who says 'No thank you; I don't drink.' "

Player Five: "Just once I'd like to see somebody write a letter to the editor of The Japan Times saying he agrees with somebody else who wrote a letter to the editor."

Anyway, on and on it went. But I'm sure you've seen enough to get the general idea of how the game goes.

Right after that particular session ended (Player Three won with; "Just once I'd like to see somebody who bought two tickets to Hong Kong and didn't win them as a door prize or at an international school bingo game"), Player One came over and asked, "Don, why don't you have a contest in the Times and offer a prize to the person who sends you the best 'Just once I'd like to see . . .' entry?"

"What sort of a prize would I give?" I asked him.

"How about first prize being an autographed copy of your book — autographed by Wife Sarah, not by you?"

"And who," I asked, "will decide who wins?"

"Wife Sarah, of course."

So, I agreed. And second and third prizes will be genuine decals that explain how to use a Western-style toilet.

You don't have to attach any chopstick wrappers or empty rice bags to your entry, but be sure you include your name and address.

Just one last thing. When I told Wife Sarah about this contest, I ended up by asking her if she really thought anybody would send in any entries.

"The ones that do," she observed, "have probably been in Japan too long."

HERE COMES THE JUDGE

I hope you read the previous article headed "Just Once I'd Like to See . . ." in which I told of a new Tokyo Parlor Game where players took a turn topping previous players' "Just Once I'd Like to See . . ." statements about Gaijin reactions to Japan. If you do recall it, you'll also remember that I announced a contest in that column for readers who would send in their "Just Once I'd Like to See . . ." entries.

Well, hundreds came in and gave Wife Sarah and I a fresh supply of smiles. Wife Sarah herself was the sole judge, and she carefully read all the entries, sorted them out, and picked the winners.

Here's *her* report in *her* words:

Right off, understand this, please: If I had my way, everyone would be a winner. But, Husband Don said nothing doing, there's only one free book and two free toilet decals to give away. To give you some idea what a tough job it was, I've made these notes on my line of reasoning:

Surprisingly enough, many, many Gaijins would just once like to see the same things. Like I couldn't even count the "Just Once, etc." entries that ended with "... people who wait until everybody else is off before they try to get on an elevator or a train."

Another one that showed up often was "... a Gaijin who doesn't complain about Japan." (There were no entries, by the way, that wanted to see a Japanese who doesn't complain about Japan.)

A good number of entries were concerned with business situations about which I'm really not familiar, so I have to admit passing over most of those. I could tell by Husband Don's reactions that some of those would have been winners if *he* were handling the judging. Sorry about that.

Two people — Ron Williams of Tokyo and Seishichi Iwakoshi of Seto — wanted to just once see a column that doesn't mention Wife Sarah. (No comments.)

A number of others caught my eye for reasons different from those previous two. Like Reg Gillmor of Hiroshima who wants to see a Japanese schoolboy decked out in a solid *white* outfit. Or Susan Gordon of Funabashi who would settle for seeing a young man give up his seat on a train to an old lady who didn't turn around and give it to her grandson.

Then there was Amy Picciano Aki of Tokushima who wants to see the reaction Clevelanders would have to plastic food displayed in a window in front of Stouffer's Restaurant in Shaker Heights. And Tokyo's Stanley Strong wants to see a piece of toast served well done, hot, and less than an inch thick. Mr. Strong is also waiting to be offered a Martini rather than more green tea.

Andrea Ishigami of Tokyo is looking for a Japanese tourist who is traveling with something more than a furoshiki for luggage. Maas Vanderbilt of Yokohama would like to see a Japanese tour group without a flag up front.

Besse Okada of Tokyo wants to see a Japanese group photo where everybody is smiling. Vladimir Brog — also from Tokyo — wants to see everybody laughing on the train. Bette and George Reese, again Tokyo, don't care whether anybody on the train is laughing; they just want to see one train traveler who's not carrying a net-bag full of Mikans.

Some — like Bette and Ken Takushi of Akishima — are looking for something as simple as 12 eggs in a plastic carton instead of the usual 10.

Many entries referred to the ecology of Japan. Carla Utech of Toyama, for instance, wants to see exactly what they do with the fish she sees them take from polluted Jinzu River everyday so she can stop imagining. Clare Baldwin of Kasugai wants to see one of those election trucks with a dead microphone.

Because I, too, would like to see everybody in Japan — natives and visitors alike — join in improving the environment, I leaned far enough toward the ecology entries to choose one of them as the First Prize Winner. It came from Eleanor Yum in Tokyo's Matsubara. Mrs. Yum said, ''Just once I'd like to see somebody being arrested for urinating on the side of the street.''

Me, too, Mrs. Yum, and so an autographed copy of Husband Don's first book (Titled: ''Japan: It's Not All Raw Fish'') will be on its way to you soon, Congratulations!

And congratulations are also in order for second prize winner Dana Slayman of Mitaka. Her entry on behalf of the cold sufferers in Japan: ''Just once I'd like to see multicolored mouth masks.'' That would cheer things up.

Third prize winner is Teasley Denison of Tokyo who

wrote, "Just once I'd like to see myself understanding all the repair man is saying without having to call my husband's secretary." I know that feeling all too well. Both Dana Slayman and Mrs. Denison will receive the Western-style toilet instruction decals.

Now, I know what all the rest of you would like to see. That's Husband Don take the writing job back from me. He will, next article.

<hr>

SOMETHING OLD, SOMETHING NEW . . .

I remember mentioning it before, so I'm sure you remember that Daughter Frances — now out of college complete with her Criminal Justice Degree and living in New York where such justice is *always* in short supply — plans to get married. The date, in fact, has been set for June 1.

Now, Daughter Frances never *was* one to snap up a lot of her father's advice and counsel, so it really came as no shock whatsoever to me when she passed up my suggestion that she elope. It didn't even move her when I guaranteed her a cash-on-elopement payment equal to 75 per cent of what the wedding would cost if she insisted on going through with it as planned.

She instead reminds me that my wedding had all the church and rice and chauffeured car and five-piece band and lavish reception ingredients that is really all she asks for herself. I've tried dozens of times to remind her that my wedding was an entirely different matter since it was Wife Sarah's father who paid for all that.

Anyway, it's going to happen in June just as it happened for Wife Sarah and I 28 years ago. Now that I finally realize the inevitability of it all, I've been brainstorming full time to figure out how I can finance all that's coming and remain partially solvent.

No luck. The wedding reception hall cartel in New York is solid.

The only thing I did come up with is an idea to make Daughter Frances' affair sort of a Japanese experience for the people back home. Because a wedding here appears to be essentially a company thing rather than a family affair, I've been invited to four or five of our employees' weddings (Wife Sarah has never been included). As a result, I think I have the routine down pat enough now to pull off a Tokyo-style ceremony in New York.

We'll probably do it something like this: First of all, we'll invite mostly home office people (without their wives). Daughter Frances can invite four or five of her girl friends — at the most — and her husband-to-be can invite a like number of his buddies.

When everybody is sitting down, Daughter Frances can come in dressed in a fancy yukata that we can pick up over in Harajuku someplace for a couple of thousand yen. New Yorkers will think it's a real kimono.

By the way, she'll march in to recorded music. That wrinkle alone will save me a fortune on a band.

After she and the groom are seated at the head table, flanked by whoever introduced them in the first place, the master of all the ceremonies will first call on some company people to make some speeches.

They'll talk about things like where and when the bride and groom were born, where they went to school, what jobs they've had. You know, talk that would make any wedding reception anywhere a real gasser.

In between all the speeches — and during some of them, in fact — older men in the group will run around among the guests competing with the waiters in pouring sake for other, red-faced, less-mobile guests. (Sake — instead of the Scotch, Gin, Tequila and Bourbon that Daughter Frances wants — will save another big bundle.)

Then, after the speeches, guests will get up one-by-one and sing songs. These will — Japanese-style — be songs from their hometowns. Like my brother — from California — will probably sing ''I Left My Heart in San Francisco.'' Daughter Frances' new father-in-law can sing, ''Sidewalks of New York,'' and somebody from the home office will certainly want to do a thing about Cleveland, but I can't remember the name of any such song at the moment. Certainly, nobody ever left their heart here.

I almost forgot. While all this is going on, the reception guests will be eating, of course. I plan to serve them rice (instead of throwing it at the newlyweds) and raw fish. They'll have to eat with chopsticks to keep the whole flavor Oriental. That's another big money-saver, since even if they like raw fish and rice, how much will they be able to eat on their maiden bout with chopsticks (especially the slippery smooth plastic ones I intend to furnish)? I don't feel we'll have to refill their bowls of miso soup or cups of green tea too often, either.

Another thing goes on during all the eating, speeching and singing. That's that Daughter Frances has to march out two or three times — to recorded music again, of course — to change into different outfits. That's OK, too. The extra clothes will cost some money, but everybody has to stand while she marches in and out. And, they can't eat or drink while they're standing. So, if she marches slowly and changes quickly, I'll be even further ahead.

One small drawback to a Japanese-style wedding is that I'll have to provide a tape-recorder. Native couples, you see, spend their post honeymoon days not only looking at the wedding picture albums, but listening to the tapes of the speeches and songs. To each his own.

And, of course, when the ceremonies are over, all the guests will follow Daughter Frances and her new husband down to the railroad station so they can clap and yell a lot of "Banzais" when the couple gets on the train — if they still have trains in New York. That ought to get a rise out of my old New York Central Railroad friends.

Just one Japanese tradition we'll skip. And that's the fact that newlyweds here always give a gift to everyone who attends the reception. That's an unnecessary expense, I feel, and New Yorkers won't even know we've left it out anyway. Unless, of course, Daughter Frances agrees to go all the way with local wedding tradition, because that would include following the practice here that the groom's father pays for everything.

Chances are, of course, that Daughter Frances won't want to go along with any of this. I don't really care, however, because one thing is certain: When I discuss this idea with her, she'll be much more reasonable about considering my offer to elope.

<hr/>

FOR BETTER OR FOR WORSE

Well, the wedding is over.

Daughter Frances is Mrs. Douglas Mangino and the couple are happily triple-locked inside their New York City West Side apartment.

94

Not only is it a relief to know that the ceremony is over, but Wife Sarah and I are practically *on* relief because of it. I still can't believe that Daughter Frances went through with it.

I mean, from what I've read in Cosmopolitan and Dear Abby lately, I thought weddings were a thing of the past. Like I thought these days that people just moved in with each other or bought a small van and drove together from the beach to the ski lift — depending on the season.

Don't misunderstand. I don't mean I'm ready to morally approve of such arrangements; I just thought that's the way it is.

Well, not with Daughter Frances and her Husband Doug. They went all the way the old way.

I remember how intrigued I was listening to her wedding plans before she left here for our old White Plains, N.Y., hometown to tie the knot.

She went into great detail about how she was going to buy a white lace gown, with veil, and with a train that sounded about as long as a Shinkansen Hikari. And how she was going to have four or five bridesmaids and a church wedding and a big dinner-reception and bands for dancing and chauffeur-driven limousines and engraved invitations and all that old Nineteenth Century stuff.

Why, she and Wife Sarah even spent hours deciding that the reception would be held down to 200 people and how Wife Sarah would wear an ivory-colored gown and how I'd give Daughter Frances away while wearing a tux with a white jacket.

Plus, Daughter Barbara would be flown from the University of Hawaii to New York so she could be maid of honor.

I said before that I was "intrigued" listening to all of this. And, I was. Until it suddenly dawned on me that *I* was the one who would finance all this intrigue.

"Hold on," I begged. "How do you think I'm going to pay for all this?"

"Really, Dad," Daughter Frances reminded, "did I ask *you* how *you* were going to pay for my college education? Of course not. And I don't think it's right to meddle into a father's finances about a wedding either."

Now it was my turn to remind. And, I started by reminding her that I hadn't *yet* paid for her college education — or, for that matter, for Son Sean's or Daughter Barbara's. I also pointed out that planning a wedding like that was about as meddling as somebody could be with my finances.

"How could you bring up money at a time like this?" Wife Sarah asked. "This is your oldest daughter's wedding we're talking about, *not* a business deal."

"That," I told Wife Sarah, "is *exactly* what I'm worried about — bringing up that much money. And, it definitely is *not* a business deal. I have to pay for all that; not put it on the expense account. We can't even charge off all the trips back to New York because this isn't a Home Leave year."

"Surely," Wife Sarah said, "the Home Office will understand and pay the air fare, anyway."

I assured her that they'd understand, but wouldn't pay the air fare unless we put off the wedding for a Home Leave year. And then held it in Cleveland, not New York.

"Out of the question," was the chorused reply.

"Well," I pleaded, "can't you at least cut down the guests down to twenty or so — just the immediate family?"

"Look," Daughter Frances explained, "You're the one who married Mom. You *knew* she was Italian, and, Doug is Italian, too."

"So?" I wondered.

"So, 200 *is* the immediate family."

"Well, why a dinner? Why not a breakfast?" I suggested.

"Whoever heard of cocktails and a band at breakfast?" Wife Sarah scoffed.

"So, kill the cocktails and band, too."

"Never."

Anyway, on and on it went. And I lost every round. Almost every round. The females did offer to forgo throwing rice at the bride and groom. All the rest went on as scheduled.

After it was all over, I was glad they won. After all, how often does one's oldest daughter get married? I mean usually, anyway?

It wasn't nearly as bad as I first thought, either. The Home Office did offer to consider my visit to the U.S. as a business trip and found plenty of business for me to do there after the wedding. And, they agreed to spring for Wife Sarah's ticket, too.

Plus, the groom paid for his own tuxedo rental and only 197 of the immediate family showed up. I told Wife Sarah, as the newlyweds took off on their honeymoon, that I was sorry I caused all the fuss and that we actually were in hock for a couple of thousand dollars less than I thought it would cost.

"Good," she sighed. "I'm glad. Because, we both need a rest and there's a cruise to Nassau we should take before we go back to Tokyo."

I started to steam up all over again, but then I thought: Why not? and, we did cruise to Nassau.

After all, Wife Sarah married me "for richer or for poorer," too.

PLEASE BUY THE BOOK

It was New Year's Day. Some friends were over for dinner, and — while we were having coffee — one of them turned and asked, "Well, Don, was 1974 a good year for the Maloneys?"

"Not bad," I said. And, we went on to another subject.

Later, I got to thinking: What kind of a year was 1974? And, I decided, "not bad" really wasn't an adequate sum-up.

First of all, Wife Sarah and I really aged in 1974, and that's somewhat depressing.

In June, we celebrated our 25th wedding anniversary.

Son Sean — who was in Tokyo for a year of study at Waseda University since the fall of 1973 — met and married a Japanese girl from Kyushu. Their joint venture produced Grandchild Miki on November 18 last. And, Son Sean was off for his U.S. Air Force training back in the United States. In Texas, anyway.

Daughter Barbara graduated from Sacred Heart High School in Tokyo last June and began her freshman year at the University of Hawaii in September.

Daughter Frances — who already has her degree from the University of Dayton and was living here with us for a year — decided to get back to New York, get a job and prepare for her upcoming wedding in June.

Son Donald, however, is still with us since he's only in eighth grade at St. Mary's in Tokyo.

So, what was a family of six in 1973 in Tokyo, scaled down to only three at home by the end of 1974.

Of course, we did gain a daughter-in-law and grandson.

Nineteen-seventy-four wasn't a banner business year for

us in Japan, either. But I'm sure I don't have to tell any of you about that.

Thanks to inflation, it seems our 1974 bills at our favorite Aoyama supermarkets to feed three were about the same as they were in 1973 to feed six.

But, 1975 started out with a couple of good omens that lead me to believe that this could be a great year.

For one thing, right after the New Year I went down to the post office to pay what I thought was our first bill of the New Year. The man wouldn't take any money. After much scrambling with the English-Japanese and Japanese-English sections of my pocket dictionary, I learned that this wasn't a bill, but a statement from the water company telling me that they overcharged me last time and I had a refund coming of ¥2,745!!

Plus, just the other day in our local shopping street, one of the storekeepers asked me to translate for this Chinese woman customer in his store who spoke no Japanese but knew some English. Imagine, he asked me to translate Japanese to English and vice versa. It turned out she wanted milk and eggs and I steered her to them. At least, that's what I think she wanted and what I told the storekeeper to give her.

It's been 26 years since Syracuse University certified me as a journalist, but just last week — finally — I completed arrangements to have my first book published.

Up to this year, the whole idea of celebrating another birthday used to upset me with its annual evidence that I was growing older. But, I had my 1975 birthday on January 6 and discovered that — once you're a grandfather — it's not possible to feel any older.

For another thing, 1975 may really be the year of the diet. Oh, there's nothing going on quite like Dr. Atkins described as his "Diet Revolution", but I'm on the way down, kilo-wise, at a steady — if not fast — pace.

And I'm sure you've noticed on FEN, that although Hiroko has started the New Year without Dan, she has no trouble understanding the new guy's Japanese. Maybe this means that, during 1975, more people will start understanding *my* Japanese.

Also, lately, I have finally mastered little things that used to cause untold problems. Like I can finally fold up my folding Japanese umbrella when I want it to fold up. And I almost never forget what I did with the little ticket when I'm about to get off the subway.

Yes, 1975 may truly be the year.

The only thing that can possibly spoil it — at least from what I can see now — will be if you don't buy the book.

HOW'S THE BOOK GOING?

No matter how the conversation starts these days, people eventually get around to asking me, "How's the Book going?"

Of course, they're referring to my first book, "Japan: It's Not All Raw Fish," and I love it. In fact, if *they* don't mention the book, *I* do. After all, that book was dozens of years in the making. It was that long between the time I finished journalism school and when the book was published last year.

I especially love the sound of the word "author" and have instructed Wife Sarah and the kids to always introduce me that way to their friends. Unfortunately, they all ignore the directive. Actually, the *only* reaction from any of them came from Son Donald who said that was the first time I told him that my real first name was "Author."

Anyway, I'm always anxious myself to know how the book is doing and I try to find out on my own every once in a while. For instance, the other day I was over at the Northwest Airlines ticket office in the Imperial Hotel, so I stopped in at the lobby bookstore. There, on the counter in front of the cashier were piles of my book and "Japan — The Fragile Superpower."

"Are these books selling well?" I asked the girl behind the counter.

"Oh, yes," she said.

"How about this one?" I asked and pointed to mine.

"It sells *very* well."

I beamed.

"It sells very well," she went on, "because ordinary people buy it. Now this one here (pointing to the other book) sells only to intellectuals, to brilliant people. Not to the *other* people who buy the Maloney book."

"Oh," I tried to smile. And, I bought one of those other books and left, completely deflated.

A few days later, I was in the Grand Palace Hotel over near my office. A home office visitor was asking about the book. I assured him it was selling very well, was about to go into the Fifth Printing, and that everybody knew about it — it was really a famous book in Tokyo.

"Maybe I should buy one and take it back to Cleveland," he offered.

"Sure," I agreed. "Come on back to the bookstore and we'll get one."

We went in but couldn't see the book anywhere. "Are you sold out of Maloney's book?" I asked the clerk.

101

"Of *whose* book?" she asked.

"Maloney's. Don Maloney's book," I repeated.

"Never heard of it. Maybe we don't carry."

"I'm sure I saw it here before," I pleaded. "It's called: Japan: It's Not All Raw Fish."

"Oh," she reacted, *"that* book. Yes, we have. It's over there on the left, in with all the other Japanese cookbooks."

The home office visitor gave me one of those understanding smiles. "Oh, these Japanese," I forced a smile of my own, "they're *always* joking."

But, it *was* with the cookbooks.

Almost everything connected with that book bursts my ego balloon. At the 30th Anniversary Ball of the Foreign Correspondents' Club of Japan, The Japan Times — publishers of the book — donated five copies of the book to be used as door prizes. When I heard that, I beamed again. "Can you imagine," I told Wife Sarah, *"my* book as a door prize at the Press Club Ball. *Five* of my books, yet."

"Maybe," Wife Sarah reasoned, "they're not selling so they're *giving* them away."

But the real fun of the book has been the autograph sessions around town. I've met a lot of readers and heard a lot of only-in-Japan stories that I'll have to tell you all about here someday.

I was especially pleased to hear from Japanese friends that they enjoyed reading the book. One even told me that another Japanese — one of his closest friends — was especially interested in the book. His friend wanted to know, he said, how many books I sold and whether or not I was making any money out of it.

"Tell him," I said — beaming again, "that the book has sold thousands and thousands and thousands of copies and that I have made more money than I ever made on any book before." I didn't think it was necessary to mention that this was my only book ever.

A few days after that exchange, I met my friend again and he wanted me to know that he'd passed on everything I'd told him to his friend. "And, he like to get some more details, if you don't mind."

"Like what?" I asked.

"Well, for instance," he said. "He wants to know *exactly* how many books were sold and *exactly* how much you made."

I could barely hide my aggravation, I mean, I'm used to it now to have Japanese ask outright questions like, "How old are you?" and so forth, but I thought this request for details on the book earnings was going too far and I said so.

"That's *private* information, don't you think?" I asked.

"I thought so, too," my friend answered, "but my friend says it isn't?"

"Who *is* this friend of yours," I wanted to know.

"I'm not sure exactly what his job is," he apologized, "but he works for the Chiyoda-Ku Tax Office."

<hr>

IV. LEISURE LIFE

Finding time for leisure pursuits in Japan is not, generally, a problem for Gaijins. Trying to figure out what to do with that leisure time, however, can be one of the biggest problems the expatriate faces.

Not that there isn't plenty to do. It's just that almost none of the usual leisure time activities are designed with the Gaijin in mind.

But, it's possible to enjoy your spare time — once you decide that you're going to while it away under different circumstances and in different areas than you've ever done it before.

And — unless you enjoy watching John Wayne speak Japanese — you'll learn to relax without television.

That opens some interesting leisure horizons. I'll give you an idea of what I mean.

ACCENTUATE THE POSITIVE

In Japan, like everywhere else — including Cleveland, I guess — transplanted persons have to struggle now and then to discover something positive to accentuate about their new home so that some portions of the negatives can be eliminated.

For example, when Wife Sarah and I were living in New York, our idea of a great night out was to take in a real live Broadway show. And, there were always dozens to choose from. In Cleveland, however, there were only a couple of legitimate theaters, and each had a fairly short season.

That's a negative, under the circumstances, for Cleveland. And, we groaned about it.

But, soon, we discovered a wonderful silver positive lining on that negative: the fact that only *good* shows made it to Cleveland. All the bad ones died in New York. Sometimes, we recalled, Wife Sarah and I had paid to attend some of those New York theater funerals. Not so in Cleveland. Fewer shows, yes; but all hits.

Then, Tokyo.

The legitimate theater negatives here for a foreigner are considerable — certainly far more than in Cleveland. But, Broadway shows *do* make it to Tokyo and, again, only the smash hits.

Of course, in Tokyo, the performances are in Japanese. Negative? Depends on how you look at it.

The other night, Wife Sarah and I went to see "Brigadoon" over at the Takarazuka Theater in Hibiya. Absolutely fascinating! It had so many negatives going for it that it wound up one of the most positive experiences we've ever had in Japan. First of all, the performance began at 5:30

106

p.m. That hour hardly allows for even *one* cocktail between the office and Hibiya, never mind a typical preshow dinner in some intimate sushi shop.

But, right inside the theater door, they sell all kinds of goodies for you to munch on during the performance. I chose an ice-cream sandwich; Wife Sarah, a bag of peanuts. And, we settled down in our almost-adequate balcony seats.

Now, as I mentioned, the dialogue was in Japanese. So were the songs. But, foreigners can rent — and we did — a little blue box, complete with earphone, that lets you listen to a simultaneous English translation of what's being said and sung on stage.

I take that back. *Sometimes* the translation is simultaneous. More often it's a little ahead or a little behind the actors on stage.

I have to take ''actors'' back, too. There are none. Not in Takarazuka, anyway. All the parts are played by girls. I have to admit that can be sukoshi distracting. I mean, the girls that play male parts dress like boys, and some of them even have deep voices. And, they all have short haircuts. But — and this is probably the most distracting part — they all *walk* like girls.

The girls that play girls are quite believable, however. They have pretty dresses, soprano voices, long hair, and walk just like the other girls that play the boys.

There's another rather serious distraction, and that brings me back to the little blue translation box. And, to be fair, I must ask you to recall that the bulk of the action in ''Brigadoon'' takes place in Scotland. And so, the dialogue, in English, is spoken with a Scottish lilt. So, naturally, that's the way the girl speaking English out of that little blue box delivered.

Now you will admit that sometimes it can be difficult to understand a Japanese person's English. At least as difficult, I imagine, as it is for a Japanese person to understand my Japanese.

Well, friends, you haven't experienced difficulty until you've heard a female Japanese voice, in English, saying lines like, ''I dinna wanna see ye this night.'' Right up to the end of the first act, until I remembered the Scotland location, I thought something was wrong with the little blue box.

Incidentally, at the end of the first — which came at 7:00 — there's a 30-minute intermission during which restaurants in the theater stand ready to serve you such Broadway favorites as sashimi and curry rice.

Wife Sarah and I skipped both.

I ask you now, where else in this world can you watch an American musical, performed by all girls, with Japanese dialogue coming in your open ear and a combination of Japanese-English-Scottish coming from a blue box into the other ear while you sit in a seat that you wear rather than occupy? While you're eating ice cream and peanuts yet.

Certainly not in New York. *Positively* not in Cleveland.

The sum total of it all makes for a unique, positive evening. Everybody should do it at least once.

After the show, Wife Sarah and I went over to the coffee shop at a nearby hotel. Our appetite had been a little dulled by peanuts, ice cream, and the second act odor of curry, so we settled on a club sandwich and a bottle of beer each. The coffee shop check came to $10.95.

That's *one* Tokyo negative for which I've *never* been able to come up with anything positive.

DON'T GO NEAR THE WATER

Whether you read the book by the same name or not, chances are far better than even that you know the movie called ''Jaws,'' which finally came to Tokyo, is about a shark. A very, *very* big shark.

I did read the book, and while I was on a home office visit in the U.S.A. last summer, I also saw the picture. And, to be perfectly honest, I wasn't crazy about the movie.

My disappointment came about, I guess, because I read the book and the movie left out so much of what I'd read and expected to see. In fact, I don't remember ever really enjoying a movie made from a book I've read.

Everything in ''Jaws'' started off about the same as I remembered the book. This wild bunch was whooping it up at somebody's beach house and one of the couples decided to go out and fool around on the beach. Or in the deep grass by the beach. Whether they actually got to do what they went out there to do is no clearer in the movie than I remember it in the book. Anyway, the guy passes out from either the late hour or the booze (or both) and the gal decides to do a moonlight skinny dip.

Enter the star of the movie, this Boeing 747 of the shark world, and gulps her down with a minimum of chomping. Actually, he doesn't gulp all of her down or there wouldn't be a book or a movie. I mean, if he ate her completely, the folks might decide she swam to Bermuda or something and forgot the whole thing. So, he — I assume he was a he, anyway — leaves just enough of her to wash up on the shore the next morning and terrify everybody around that beach town.

That's what she gets, I thought, for going in naked. And

— 109 —

at night, yet. If she wore her suit, I thought, the shark wouldn't have been interested at all.

But, that theory didn't hold water. Because, in the next day or so — in broad daylight — the shark eats a kid in a standard bathing suit. He even ate part of the rubber raft the kid was playing on. And before the movie ends, he eats one of the fully-clothed human stars, Robert Shaw, who wasn't even in the water at the time, but in his boat!

One of the main threads of the story is that the town fathers of this little Long Island beach community where all this happens don't want the word to get out that a giant shark is eating everybody. If word does leak, they fear nobody will come for the summer season and what would the local shopkeepers do with all those hot dogs, cotton candy, custard cones, beach balls and T-shirts with porno iron-ons on the front?

In the book, I went along with that reasoning. But, while watching the movie, I decided they were 100 per cent wrong. They should have bought prime time on TV commercials to tell the world that this giant shark was eating all these kids and skinny dippers.

Why, when I saw ''Jaws'' in Fort Lauderdale last summer, the lines went around the theater two or three times. Some had to stand in those lines three or four hours just to see a movie about a shark eating people. Imagine how many people would flock to some beach town for a chance at seeing a real shark eat some real people. They'd have run out of cotton candy by June 30!

Besides, beach towns don't make money from the people who are swimming, anyway. They make money from the nonswimmers who are down on Main Street spending their traveler's checks. And let me tell you, while ''Jaws'' was showing at the local movie houses, that's where people in Ft. Lauderdale were — on Main Street, not on the beaches. The few that were on the beaches never went in the water over their toenails. They weren't even swimming in hotel pools if they were filled with salt water.

Of course, "Jaws" won't have quite the same effect on the Japanese people who see it. For one thing, it's showing here in the dead of winter — not in summer — and nobody is at the beach, anyway.

For another thing, even if it was summer, I doubt any harm could be done. If you've ever been to a Japanese beach in the summer, you know why I say that. So many people are in the water around here then that there's no room for a pollywog, much less a shark. In fact, if they made a movie about Japanese beaches and showed it to the sharks, the sharks would be afraid to stay in the water.

But back to why I never like movies made from books — and to "Jaws" in particular. In the book, the beach town policeman who tries to catch the big shark invites a young shark specialist down from somewhere near Boston to help. Before this specialist ever gets around to subduing the shark in the book, he subdues the wife of the policeman in a local motel.

So, all during the movie, I'm watching them both, waiting for the specialist to make his motel move. It never comes and the distraction of waiting for it made me miss most of the movie.

But, I guess maybe there's some sort of moral lesson intended. You see, in the book where the near-Boston guy does score with Mrs. Policeman, the shark eats him in the end. In the movie, where he never gives her more than a "Konnichiwa," he escapes the shark.

Anyway, considering what else there is to do around here during the upcoming holiday season, you might as well go see "Jaws." If you get nothing else out of the movie, you'll certainly enjoy the switcheroo involved. And that comes from the fact that you're now in a country where almost any time of any day you can see people eating raw fish.

In "Jaws," you'll get a chance to see a fish eat some raw people.

A MODERN TALE OF GENJI

One of the very real problems a transplanted American faces in Japan is organizing an "eating out" evening with the family. At least that's true for my ex-Cleveland family.

There are two hurdles that have to be overcome. First, I guess, is the fact that most Americans — and my family in particular — are convinced that most Japanese food is served while it's still moving.

It was easy for my brood to get that impression since the first Japanese meal ever served us was a bowl of rice with live shrimp dancing around on top. I'll never forget how difficult it was to chopstick some of the comparatively docile rice while avoiding the rather active shrimp. I tried to immobilize my shrimp with soy sauce, but it only seemed to act like the elixir of crustacean youth, turning what was only a Fox Trot up to then into what I remembered from my high school days as a "Lindy."

Wife Sarah and the kids fared much better by just smiling through the whole thing and concentrating on an assortment of pickled something-or-others that reclined rather peacefully in an accompanying dish.

Our next bout with Japanese food came a few weeks later when a native host down in Kyushu honored our choice of fish over meat and took us to a place in Hakata City that looked like a branch of the old aquarium that used to be in New York's Battery Park.

A U-shaped counter in that restaurant nearly surrounded a pool inhabited by quite-alive fish of all sorts of shape and sizes. "How about Red Snapper?" our host asked.

"Why not?" I answered for all.

In a very few minutes, I found out exactly why not. Our benefactor pointed to what was undeniably a fish we Clevelanders call Red Snapper. A man standing alongside the pool — with that official fish restaurant towel wrapped around his head — netted out the designated fish, flipped it to a waiting swordsman posted at the head of the "U" who sliced up one side of the fish into pieces about as thick as this page you're reading, put everything on a blue plate, and sent it back to our seat.

Because the swordsman exercised extreme care, the fish was still very much alive on arrival and opened and closed his mouth in the manner you expect of such fish, even though the shavings of his right side were piled up like Mt. Fuji.

Our host pointed to still-snapping Snapper and said, "Go ahead."

Don't ask me how, but I did. What made it possible, I think, was the fact that I was able to casually drop the paper wrapper from my chopsticks so that it covered the Snapper's great big eye and gasping mouth.

Wife Sarah and the kids ate just enough to hold them over until we returned to our hotel and the more familiar cucumber goodies that room service delivers — even in Hakata City.

The other hurdle involved in organizing a dinner out — Japanese style — is the fact that most Japanese restaurants specialize, with a capital "S". In other words, sushi restaurants serve *only* raw fish on rice, tempura restaurants

113

offer *only* batter-dipped, deep-fried everything and soba shops concentrate on dozens of varieties of the same basic noodle.

Now it's tough enough in my house to get everybody to agree on the same *night* for a dining out. And with that accomplished it's almost impossible to get them all to agree on the same main dish or variety thereof.

As a result, we would normally choose a so-called Western-style restaurant which generally offers a chance at their choice of entree, be it fish, fowl, or four-legged origin.

But, while you're in Tokyo, there are some Japanese restaurants you *must* try. Like ''Tonki's'' near Meguro Station. There, you can get a full-course filet pork cutlet dinner (Tonkatsu) for less than a drink costs in many places. And, full-course *includes* soup, salad, rice and pickled something-or-other. Plus, the best show in town just watching all this prepared in front of you.

And there must be thousands of tempura restaurants around town like the one near our office that serves the soup-to-pickles lunch for less than the price of 37 grapes at Kinokuniya.

Or how about trying the best 4,000 of the one million soba shops in town where you can have lunch for what you'd pay for a pack of Seven Stars, and formal dinners — including Pepsi — for only a few yen more.

Of course, the prices at either ''Tonki's'' or the tempura place doesn't include napkins. But, you can't have *everything*. And the soba shops do *not* pay the cost of medical care required to repair your knee-caps which will almost certainly be shattered when they strike that rack that is built-in — for some reason or other — under every table in every soba shop I've ever visited. But, chances are, even if you had your knees replaced by one of the top knee surgeons in Tokyo, the total bill for soba *and* new knees would be less than the check from many of the restaurants that boast ''Western-Style'' menus.

114

And, please try McDonald's, Kentucky Fried Chicken, Anna Miller's, Dunkin' Donuts, Shakey's Pizza Parlor, Pizza Hut, A&W Root Beer, Dairy Queen, or any other such all-American spots where you can not only get food you can recognize from similar places back in Cleveland, but you *do* get napkins, and can be virtually assured that your knees will completely survive the meal.

And, you must also sample one of the best lunches in Tokyo. I do it every once in a while and enjoy every minute of it — including the food. Directions on how to pull this particular experience off are rather simple:

Go down to Tokyo Station and buy a ''platform ticket.'' Go upstairs onto any track where the Shinkansen (or Bullet Trains) come and go. There, you'll find stands that sell those ''Obentos'' — or Japanese box lunches.

Be careful, because those stands sell many varieties of Obentos and I'd hate to see you get involved in the wrong one. Ask for the one that includes an hors d'oeuvre of salami, cheese and pickle, plus a rather generous sandwich. *And* a half-bottle of rose wine with a plastic wine glass. You'll have precious little problem ordering it since they call it — in Japanese — ''Wine Obento.'' It costs only a few hundred yen for everything, even the moist towel, napkin and personal toothpick.

Then, sit down on one of the platform chairs and watch the people pushing each other on and off the bullet trains. It's a special kind of pleasure when you know *you're* not going anywhere.

In what other city in the world can you see a show *and* lunch like that? Outdoors, yet.

When you're ready to go first class on Japanese food, try Genji, the Japanese restaurant in Tokyo Hilton Hotel. It's our favorite non-Western eat-out spot.

For one thing, it offers a wide variety of food Japanese. And, let's face it, the Japanese know Japanese food best. In other words, it's safe to say that a *bad* Japanese Japanese restaurant serves more interesting food than a *good* Japanese Western-style spot. Just, by the way, as the same is true in reverse back in Cleveland, Ohio.

Here's just some of the things Genji has going for it:

First off, variety. Everything from soup — and two kinds of that — to sashimi. If you prefer your fish cooked, it's there. So is good old fried chicken — chopstick-lickin' good. If you're not sure exactly what kind of Japanese food to try, an hors d'oeuvres assortment gives you a chance to try most all of it and make up your own mind.

Secondly, all the traditional safe-for-foreigners food like Suki-yaki and Shabu Shabu are on the daily menu, too. So is my favorite, a thing called Ishiyaki. That's a combination of Kobe Beef, Scallops and Chicken grilled to perfection on, of all things, a red-hot stone and served up with an assortment of hors d'oeuvres, Salad, Soup, Rice and Pickles.

And not to be overlooked is the fact that Genji has its menus printed in my favorite English with explanations that prevent any surprises like dancing shrimp.

While you can go Japanese all-the-way and begin and end your meal with Sake, it's reassuring to know that Genji knows how to put together the best Martinis and Manhattans this side of the International Date Line.

Even with all this, however, probably the number one asset of Genji is that you can do all these native things while you're sitting in a chair — *not* on the floor.

By the way, some of the most moving stories of old Japan — fifty-four of them to be exact — are included in a very famous volume entitled "Tales of Genji" which is where the restaurant got its name.

In this modern Hilton Genji, however, nothing is moving unless you order it that way.

☙☙☙☙☙☙☙☙☙☙☙☙☙☙☙☙☙☙☙☙

MAFIA-SAN

Sometime last year, I remember reading about a movie that was being made here about the "Yakuza," a group that was described then as sort of an Oriental version of the "Mafia."

Now, thanks to movies like "The Godfather" and books like "The Valachi Papers," I'm quite familiar with Mafia lore and could hardly wait to see this Yakuza movie.

Like I thought about the scene in "The Godfather" where they all came over to Marlon Brando's house and his wife cooked up a big pot of spaghetti and meatballs for everybody. I was anxious to see the Japanese version where, I imagined, everybody would be coming over to the leader's house and Mrs. Mafia-San would be whipping up tons of soba or slicing up dozens of raw squid for the gang.

And, I imagined, while everybody in "The Godfather" was shot in some fancy Italian restaurant or other, the Japanese version would probably show the victims being karate chopped in half while standing up eating yakitori at some open-air stand near Meiji Shrine.

Godfather Marlon Brando, I recalled, was whisked all over Brooklyn and Long Island in his big white-walled Cadillac. I was sure his Asian counterpart would be driven around on white slipcovers in the back of a black hired car.

Well, I'm sorry to report, it was nothing like that in "The Yakuza" movie.

117

In fact, there wasn't even one scene of anybody collecting protection money from a sake shop.

Let me tell you what I did see in the movie. If I give away the plot, it is purely unintentional — believe me — since I don't think there was one.

The whole thing started off with this Gaijin who lives here in Japan and had his daughter kidnapped by the Yakuza. He came asking some guy in California (it looked like California, anyway) to make a trip to Japan to help him get his daughter back. It seems the Yakuza took his daughter because he didn't smuggle them any guns like he promised — and already collected for.

The Gaijin was played by Brian Keith and the California guy by Robert Mitchum. Keith was hard to believe. I mean he didn't smoke Seven Stars, or say "Ah so desu ka," or bow when he met Mitchum, or anything authentic like that. He never even asked Mitchum what company he was with or brought him a gift.

Mitchum was OK. He, you find out, was here in Japan long ago with the occupation forces. During that time (he looked like an old MP, by the way) he saved a Japanese girl and her daughter from a fire and moved in with them for a while after that — in a version of off-base housing, I guess. Her Japanese brother didn't like it even sukoshi when he came back from the war and found his sister shacked-up with Mitchum. But, he didn't raise any fuss because Mitchum did, after all, save her life.

Now you know right away that this brother is not her brother, but her Japanese husband. You can tell that right off the way he ignores her. But Mitchum doesn't catch on until the end of the movie.

Incidentally, the guy who plays the brother/husband is Ken Takakura, a really good actor for a non-Gaijin. Those of us

118

who are paired up with really sharp Japanese counterparts in our joint ventures will know exactly how Mitchum will feel when he sees this picture. Or when his boss does.

Anyway, Mitchum and Takakura set up a 50/50 joint venture to get the daughter back for Brian Keith. Takakura has to help Mitchum because of the saving-the-sister-from-the-fire obligation, you see.

They find out where the Yakuza fellows are keeping the daughter because Takakura was once a Yakuza man himself, but he gave it up.

Two things about it that bothered me. First off, the inference was that life-long employment is no longer true in Japan since he changed jobs. Second thing, he supposedly went "straight," but Mitchum finds him in one of those schools teaching young Japanese kids how to beat each other up with those long sticks.

But, back to the action. Mitchum is all for shooting these Yakuza guys, but Takakura-San says no soap, because Japanese can only kill other Japanese with swords in a deal like this. Right then I wondered why the hell the Yakuza wanted to buy the guns from Keith in the first place.

Unless it was to shoot Gaijins, and that made me nervous.

It really doesn't matter, because just before he saves Keith's daughter, Mitchum goes and shoots Keith very dead in his Tokyo office for some double-cross reason I never understood.

Takakura-San sticks to his sword story and cuts up a subway car full of guys in one room, who — don't ask me why — waited their one-by-one turn to be sliced just like others do on those TV samurai movies. I mean, why the umpteen bad guys never attack the lone good guy all at once, I'll never know.

I already told you the end. You can assume that brother

Takakura goes back to being husband Takakura again, because Mitchum goes home to California.

But, go see "The Yakuza" anyway. Don't let the lack of realism upset you. Just because Mitchum doesn't have any trouble with Haneda customs, never gets lost, is not once passed up by a taxi, and doesn't complain about Tokyo prices — don't feel cheated.

You will hear Mitchum speak some Japanese, and that alone is worth the price of admission.

Because, you'll feel much better about yours.

DEAD GIVEAWAY

Say what you want about Cleveland — and, much to the chagrin of the Chamber of Commerce there, most people do — but you have a choice of all sorts of things to do there on a given Saturday night.

In Tokyo, it's different. On most Saturday nights, there's nothing. On precious few Saturdays, there's a chance to attend one of the parties thrown here by the schools or clubs.

Personally, I thought one such party "Hong Kong Night" at the Tokyo American Club some time ago, was a smash hit. If you passed it up — but from the looks of the crowd in the American Room that night, not many did — you really missed a great evening.

I mean, everything was quite authentically Hong Kong. Like there was plenty of Chinese food at the buffet tables — l-o-v-e those buffets! — but, an hour after I ate, I was hungry again. The entertainment was imported from the British Crown

Colony, too. Why I even heard the next morning at Sunday brunch that three couples who attended the party were in bed with Hong Kong Flu.

The only thing about it, in fact, that wasn't *thoroughly* Hong Kong was that nobody had a chance to argue over the price when they were picking up their tickets for the event.

The only low spot of the whole night, to tell the truth, was the inevitable door prize drawings. Now before I go on, I must tell you that I didn't win anything. And, that I almost never do at one of these things. I say I must tell you that because you may wish to decide that's why I hate the giveaway part of Tokyo nights out.

But, believe me, that's not the reason. In fact, it could have been worse on Hong Kong night to win something — like a Hong Kong guidebook in Japanese.

It's not that I don't appreciate the contribution of valuable prizes by generous merchants and manufacturers. I do.

It's just that I think it's so silly to waste all that good dancing, drinking, and dialogue time calling numbers.

What with American Club, Chamber of Commerce, school, church, and miscellaneous association annual balls and regular parties that I love to attend — and do — I'll bet I've already spent a cumulative total of two and a half months of my Tokyo stay listening to somebody call raffle numbers. Or, even worse than that, calling those numbers myself.

I've watched at least 147 people run up with the other half of a ticket that won them round-trips for two to Hong Kong (space available). If a woman goes up to collect the tickets — along with a flight bag usually still wrapped in plastic like the inside of a Toyota — she really squeals with joy. The husband, on the other hand, never squeals. That's because he knows that even if the tickets *are* free, and even if the Hilton *does* throw in

121

four days and three nights (or is it vice-versa?), the money his Okusan will spend shopping down there could easily wipe him out more handily than a free trip to Kinokuniya.

Incidentally, I was really surprised to learn from a friend at Northwest Airlines the other day that Gaijins in Japan *can* buy tickets to Hong Kong from the airlines. I thought you *had* to win them or you couldn't go.

So, what I'm after with all this to convince any of you who might be involved in the future serving on a committee that's running a dance, ball or party — and you're *going* to be involved, you *know* that — hold out for a no-door-prize night. Argue that the people really came to eat, dance, drink, talk and have a general good time and *not* to send one squealer home with space-available tickets to bankruptcy.

Of course, if you *really* think people only come to hear somebody call the numbers, why not save all the door prizes from all the dances held by Gaijin groups in Tokyo and have one giant nothing-but-numbers-calling night in Korakuen Stadium on the last Sunday of each month.

Or else, pull the numbers out in the cloak room and notify the winners by mail.

The only strong objections to all this, I hope, will come from the musicians' union. I'm sure they prefer the forty-five minutes of drum-the-drawings to playing the dance music they were hired to play.

And don't misunderstand me. I'm *not* talking about Bingo nights around town — just dances and parties. After all, when people go to a Bingo night, they fully expect to spend an evening listening to somebody call numbers. And, to cover their whole card before anybody else does and so wind up in Hong Kong for four days and three nights.

Someday, there may be some sort of a no-raffle night for

Gaijins in Tokyo. In the meantime, don't lose the other half of your ticket.

GOOD EVENING; IT'S MORNING

There's a whole list of things that — while I never had any of them back in Cleveland — I'd be lost without in Tokyo.

Like take those two mirrors out on the front fenders of my car. When they first delivered my car, I tried — in the interest of saving a few yen — to get the dealer to leave off the mirrors. I explained how I'd been driving umpteen years in America without them. The ordinary rearview mirror inside the car, I insisted, was perfectly adequate.

The dealer listened. He said, "Hai." And, of course, delivered the car complete with fender mirrors anyway.

God bless him! (Although, I admit, that wasn't what I asked God to do at the time.) Other cars, as I'm sure you know, come at you in Japan from all angles and from every direction. A mirror on each fender is not only mandatory for traffic survival, but only two may not be enough.

Anyway, what I'm getting at is that I need those Japanese things.

Another thing I need ("thing" doesn't really seem to be the word I'm looking for) in Japan is FEN, the U.S. Military Radio Station. And so, I wish they would stop trying their damnedest to make me stop listening to it. This "they" being whoever decides the programming at FEN.

Now, first off, let me freely admit that I fully understand that FEN is not in Japan for my personal benefit. Neither is it for me alone that somebody came up with the fender mirrors.

123

But, I certainly enjoy those mirrors. And, I want to keep enjoying FEN.

Despite the things they've done over the past few months to upset the normal program routine on FEN, I've remained silent. I can do so no longer.

For instance, I didn't write my Congressman when ''Chicken Man'' disappeared from the radio. But, I certainly wanted to. To me, it wasn't just another program. To me, ''Chicken Man'' himself was the foreign businessman in Japan.

The police commissioner represented all those forces in Japan that seem determined to insure that the foreign businessman here never gets to do his thing right, no matter how valiant his fight or how altruistic his goals.

And, that nasal-voiced Miss Helsinger was every bilingual Japanese secretary I ever met, ever-trying to explain ''Chicken Man's'' world to the police commissioner's world, and vice-versa, while all the time realizing neither would *ever* understand the other. I knew ''Chicken Man'' would never win — even with his mother's help (his mother was the home office, of course), but that's why I identified.

Then, bing. ''Chicken Man'' disappears like a slurped noodle in a soba shop. No ''gomen nasai'' from the military. Nothing. Just bing.

Oh, they tried with ''Tooth Fairy.'' But, nothing. I can't possibly identify there. In my four years in Japan, nobody ever left anything under my pillow. Besides, in Japan, you don't remove bad teeth, you gold-plate them.

Next, Dan disappears. After all those years of working on him every morning and afternoon, Hiroko gets stuck with a brand-new Gaijin who can't even ''Kore'' his ''hon desu.''

I was more than somewhat upset. I know I'll never understand Hiroko's Japanese. It's much too authentic. But, I was just getting around to understanding Dan's Nihongo. Then, another bing. This new Gaijin.

Oh, I suppose someday I'll get to understand the new guy's Nihongo, too. But, I don't have the same confidence about his English, so I may never know what his Nihongo words mean.

Then, still another FEN bing. That morning — morning, remember — I woke up to the guy on the 7 o'clock news saying "Good Evening, this is (I forget the name) from New York with tonight's news. . ."

And, this person — he wasn't a Navy journalist, or an Air Force sergeant, or a Marine corporal or anything authentic like that — then proceeded to gallop thru the news. Oh, he stopped long enough for another guy to give a warning that dogs were going to sniff your baggage at customs from now on, but he quickly resumed the gallop. You should have heard the funny way he pronounced the names of people and places in the news. Funny compared to old FEN stand-bys, anyway.

And, he never once mentioned where the previous night's Tokyo earthquake registered on the Japanese scale of seven. All he talked about was that other world.

Just before he ended, I thought: "Don't tell me he's going to give the New York weather forecast for last night, too." But, he didn't. A familiar voice cut in with the 20th Weather Squadron's promise for the day. And, they were especially accurate that morning. They predicted rain for Tokyo and fair skies for Sasebo. Well, it rained in Sasebo and was beautiful in Tokyo. The weather was right; only the cities were wrong.

Hopefully, this news-from-afar thing is only a test for two months, like FEN says.

And, equally hopefully, we'll soon get back to local news-casters who can pronounce names the way they taught me so that I can understand what's going on where and to whom.

And, along with the local newscaster, I hope they bring back ''Chicken Man'' and Dan, too.

If not, I'm switching to short-wave BBC. I won't understand their pronunciations, either, and I'll never know where the Officer's Wives' Club is having their next bazaar. But, everything will sound like it's coming from inside a barrel instead of just the newscasts and the live basketball games.

V. BUSINESS IS BUSINESS

One of the more serious culture shocks experienced by the Gaijin businessman surfaces when he realizes that although business is still business in Japan, the way they *do* business is more than somewhat different.

And it really hurts when we foreign giants of industry suddenly realize — and we *all* do, sooner or later — that we have something to *learn* about doing business. It hurts, because we all came here to *teach* how business is done, *not* to learn.

But, learn we do. And, once we learn that we're going to do some learning, it can actually be fun doing business.

First, however — just like playing any game — you have to understand the rules. Not *agree* with the rules, just *understand* them.

THE YEN IS UP BECAUSE IT'S DOWN

"Did you see this story?" Wife Sarah asked, concentrating on the upper left hand corner of The Japan Times front page the other day. Before I could answer she continued, "It says the yen is going up. Now we can get ¥304 for a dollar."

"You'd better read the story again," I suggested. "Either the yen is going up, or we can get ¥304 for a dollar. It can't be both."

"Why not?" she asked. "Last week I only got ¥296 for each dollar. Now, I can get ¥304. That's going up, isn't it?"

I assured her that such a situation was, indeed, indicative of something going up. But, I explained, "The dollar is what's going up, not the yen. The yen is obviously going down if you can get ¥304 now for what you used to get only ¥296 for."

"How," she asked, "is the yen going down when I get more of them than I used to?"

"That is," I described mistakenly, "a simple matter to explain."

"Start explaining," Wife Sarah directed as she folded the paper.

"Well," I started, "it's like this: When there's only a few dollars around and a lot of yen, yen goes down. . ."

"Down from ¥304 to ¥296?" she interrupted.

"Down from ¥296 to ¥304," I corrected.

"There you go again. Even in Japan, everyone knows ¥296 to ¥304 is up, and ¥304 to ¥296 is down. Even if we're talking about yen, up is up, down is down," Wife Sarah insisted.

"Well, that's just not true. Look, Sarah, if today a Tokyo

130

supermarket was selling 296 apples for a dollar, and then next week sold apples at 304 for a dollar — eight more apples than they gave you for a dollar today — wouldn't you say the price of apples was going down?''

"That doesn't make any sense at all.''

"Why not?''

"Because no Tokyo supermarket would ever sell 296 of anything for a dollar — even yen. And, of course, the apples *would* be cheaper next week if they were still the same apples that were around last week. But actually, it would be more like apples were ¥304 *each* today, and only ¥296 *each* next week. *That's* going down.''

I decided to take a new tack. "Look, Sarah, forget about the apples.''

"*You're* the one who wanted to buy the apples,'' she reminded. "I was talking about yen.''

"OK, OK,'' I agreed. "Here's what happened to the yen: Business people need more dollars this week to pay import bills than they have needed for a long time, and so they have to pay more yen to get each one. That's why the price of dollars went up. Right now, people with yen need dollars.''

"But, we're people with dollars, and it seems to me we need more yen every week but get less — unless we give them more dollars.''

"Up to now, yes. But, as you can see from the paper, you'll now get more yen because of the dollar shortage.''

Now Wife Sarah stood up. "We've always had a dollar shortage — ever since we arrived here — and the shorter our dollars got, the less yen we received for them. You're all mixed up. Don't you remember when they gave us ¥360 for each dollar? Now, even if you're right and the yen is going up, it's still down from ¥360.'' Satisfied that she was the victor, Wife Sarah sat down again.

For some reason I'll never understand, I decided to take one more stab at it. Without the apples.

"Sarah, now listen carefully, please. The yen is cheaper now than last week. We don't have to pay one dollar now for ¥296. We only have to pay about 98 cents for ¥296. That's down, isn't it?"

She smiled. *"That,* I understand. But, I wish it would have settled at ¥300 for a dollar, it used to be so simple for me to figure out how much everything here was really costing in dollars. I just divided the yen price tag by three and forget some zeros. Now, I'll have to divide the yen price by 296, and even that will only give me the dollar price by 98 cents worth and I'll have to divide or multiply by something again to turn the 98 cents into dollars."

"Sarah, *please,"* I begged. "Forget about the whole thing. Go to the bank and ask them to explain it to you."

"You're angry. How can you be angry when we're going to get more yen for our dollars? Now we'll be able to buy the imported food you like cheaper."

"No, we won't," I stopped her. "Don't you see, the importers will now have to pay more yen for each dollar's worth of food they import. So, the price here will go up. Only Japanese food exported to the rest of the world will get cheaper."

"You're right," she decided. "I'll ask the bank to explain it. You only mix me up. Can I get anything for you at the bank?"

"Yes, please get me some yen. As many yen as five dollars will buy."

"What," she asked, "will you do with only five dollars worth of yen?"

"I want it in brand-new one yen coins. Five bucks should get me about 1,520 one yen coins. We'll use them when we play poker instead of chips. You couldn't ever buy 304 chips for a dollar, anywhere.''

''Sure, you could,'' Wife Sarah was confident.

''Where?''

''Same place you got 294 apples for a dollar.''

<hr />

YAMAMOTO'S RULES OF ORDER

Doing business in Japan occasionally involves actually leaving the office. But mostly, business here centers around attending meetings. Even on those occasions when you actually leave the office, it's usually just to go to a meeting somewhere else.

Meetings in Japan, in fact, are held in many different places, in many different kinds of atmosphere, and for many different reasons. But, the rules under which the meetings are held seldom vary.

Probably the most important thing for newcoming businessmen to understand right off is that one thing meetings *never* do in Japan is reach a definitive decision about anything. Except, perhaps, when and where the next meeting will be.

The most you can ever expect from a business meeting is a sort of confirmation of agreements already reached as a result of countless other meetings at much lower levels.

And also understand this: just two people can never have a meeting. A conversation, yes. But genuine meetings require scores of people — many of whom you've never seen before, and most of whom you'll never see again. Take as many people you like from your side to a meeting; the other side will bring even more.

As soon as you enter the meeting room, you'll know where you stand at any particular meeting — at least where you stand in the eyes of the guy who holds the door. Notice he'll "dozo" people inside the meeting room in a very special order. First guy in: Top Dog. Last guy in: The one who carries all the brief cases.

Where you sit during a meeting is extremely important. If you're directed to an armchair with the back to a window or the back to that little alcove where the host company president's wife shows off her Ikebana, you're doing fine. If you're told to share a couch with your back to the door, you probably should have stayed home.

Despite the order of entering the room and the location of your seat, the Japanese pull one more security check on meeting goers and that's business card inspection. You must give one of your cards to, and take one of theirs from, everybody in the room that you're meeting with for the first time. There's still a death sentence in Japan and it's for people who offer business cards to, or accept business cards from, people they have already met sometime before.

So, be careful. Chances are they all look alike to you, but you don't look alike to them. Safest thing, I find, is just to smile and not stick out a business card to anybody who doesn't stick out his to me. It'll take many meetings before you learn how to smoothly take a business card from someone at the same instant that you're handing yours to him, but just watch how the natives do it and you'll eventually get with it.

One more thing about business cards: You must *stand* and bow to take or give one, *never* in a sitting position. That's not as simple as it sounds, either, because although the seats in an average Japanese meeting room look like seats, they are only pillow-high and not easy to leave once you're settled in. Sort of

134

sit on the edge until you're sure everyone who's coming has arrived.

Japanese meetings, by the way, are split into three parts. First, there's the arrival ceremonies with the business cards. Then, there's endless talk about things that have nothing to do with what you thought was going to happen at the meeting, and then there's the part where silence reigns for a few minutes, and — suddenly — it's all over.

During that first part, certain things have to be established, and the quicker and clearer you answer all the questions, the sooner you can leave and go to your next meeting.

Questions that require direct answers include: "How long have you been in Japan?" "When will you return home?" "Have you ever seen Mt. Fuji?" and, "Do you like Japanese sushi?"

Answer the first three anyway you like, but watch that fourth one — especially if lunch is part of or is to follow the meeting. Because, if you're one of those people who believes you have to tell Japanese people only wonderful things about Japan and — following such a code of behavior — tell your questioner you L-O-V-E Japanese sushi, *that's* what you're going to get for lunch. Tons of it. So better to be honest, even if it *is* a business meeting.

You ask some questions, too, just to justify your presence at the meeting. Like ask somebody on the other side: "Have you ever been to the United States (or wherever you're from)?" "When are you going to visit again (only if his answer to the first one was affirmative, of course)?" "Have you ever seen Niagara Falls (or the Tower of London, or Eiffel Tower, or the Coliseum, etc. — again, depending on where you are from)?" And, ask him if *he* likes Japanese sushi. Maybe you'll be lucky, who knows?

135

Notice that at most meetings, the attendees are never anything like the people you meet on trains, in subways, or escalators — people who want to practice English conversation. Nobody but *nobody* in a Japanese meeting wants to practice English, so you'll only know what the interpreter wants to tell you. And he may even do some editing on his own — particularly on the way you answer the sushi question. Better bring your own interpreter, by the way. And someone on whom you have something, like an employee of your home office to whom you owe money. Even then, you'll find out little enough about what's going on and much, much less if he's not on your side.

There's much more to tell you, but it will have to wait. My secretary just told me I have to leave now.

I'm going to another meeting.

<hr />

MORE ABOUT MEETINGS

In the previous article, I told you some of the things you'll need to know about how to conduct yourself at a Japanese business meeting and how to understand what's going on. I'll pick right up where I left off.

While the opening questions are being asked and answered at such a meeting, line up the business cards you collected on the table in front of you and take out your cigarettes and lighter and lay them next to the lined-up cards.

Even if you don't smoke, bring cigarettes. They are an extremely important tool at a Japanese meeting and no meeting can end without them. I'll get to that in a minute.

First real action you should take at any local meeting is to offer, to all those within arm's length, a cigarette. Japanese will generally hold up a hand, wave it back and forth slightly in front of your cigarette pack in a motion that will lead you to believe he doesn't want one. But, just as you then pull your pack back, he'll grab one anyway. I'm not sure what that waving means, but watch what the winning sumo wrestlers do on TV just before they grab that envelop from the referee and you'll see what I'm talking about.

If it's a good day for you, the people you offer cigarettes to will *really* decline (with much the same waving motion, by the way). I say "Good Day," because if they accept your offer, later you'll have to accept a cigarette offer from them. And, mark my words, it's *always* a "Peace" or "Hope" you have to take.

While you're smoking at a meeting, don't put your cigarettes too close to the ashtray when you're flicking off your ashes. If you do, especially in the opening minutes of a meeting, you'll hear a hissing sound much like the way air passes through the clenched teeth of a taxi driver when you hand him a map with only English writing.

But the meeting hiss is quite different compared to the taxi hiss. It means your cigarette came too close to the ashtray and the glowing end was doused by the water that's always in the bottom of a meeting room ashtray. As I said, this usually happens only in the beginning of a meeting. Since only chain smokers are invited to meetings in Japan, the ashtray fills right away with soggy butts.

Now I can imagine how you feel about green tea, but don't ever refuse it at a meeting. If you do, they're liable to bring you coffee instead. And, believe me, compared to any coffee I've ever been served at a Japanese meeting, the *worst* cup of green tea tastes like Mumm's Cordon Rouge 1949.

137

As soon as the tea is delivered — and that girl who delivers it says whatever it is she says as she puts it down on your lined-up business cards — take out a little black book and a pen. Everybody else will. And, by the way, don't be afraid to ignore the tea girl. I mean no one else will thank her or smile at her or anything. Don't you, either. You'll spoil the whole meeting.

But back to the little black book. Everytime somebody besides you speaks, write something in the book. Watch the others when you talk and you'll see what I mean. I'm not sure *what* you should write in the book exactly, anymore than I know what *they're* writing in their books. But *write*. I think what they're doing is taking notes for another meeting I'm sure they have after I leave.

Notice, unlike our usual ''Don't-disturb-me-during-a-meeting'' rule back home, every Japanese will, at some time or other during a meeting, be called out. I don't know whether he goes to change a tape on a recorder somewhere or just ducks out to wash down his green tea with a Pepsi. But, each will disappear for a time.

And don't be surprised that even though dozens come to a meeting, only one or two does all the talking. The rest are there just to nod and say ''Hai'' so the speaker knows when each of his sentences ends.

By the way, I almost forgot to tell you why you leave the cigarette pack and your lighter on the table all during the meeting.

Notice next time that the only way you can tell when a Japanese meeting is over is when whoever called it in the first place picks up his cigarettes, his lighter, his little black book and his lined-up business cards and puts them in his pocket. You do the same, because *that's* the end. Sometimes, at informal meetings, there's no business cards *or* black books, so

138

always watch the cigarettes and lighter. They are always there.

I remember one time back in the U.S. — during a Chicago printers convention, in fact — dozens of us were jammed into a Conrad Hilton Hotel elevator after a night of typical convention-type revelry. The last guy in was so jammed, he couldn't even turn around and was facing all the rest of us. With his tie askew, his jacket off one shoulder, he blinked his very red eyes and slurred, ''I suppose you're all wondering why I called this meeting.''

I wonder the same thing here every day.

But, the worst part often comes long after the meeting ends. It comes about two in the morning next day when the telephone ringing jolts you out of a sound sleep and the home office voice on the other end asks, ''What happened at the meeting today?''

How can you tell him that you haven't yet figured that out for yourself?

POVERTY BEGINS AT HOME

From Cambridge, Mass., a few weeks back came a report put together by the Harvard-MIT Joint Center for Urban Studies that said — despite what they might profess in public — Americans are, indeed, class conscious, and they judge others by how much money they have and how they spend it.

The man who did the study talked to 900 Americans and found that they classed the public into seven economic and social layers based on income. Those layers, and the annual incomes that identified them, went like this:

Top was the "Success Elite," with $50,000 or more. Next was the "Doing Very Well" layer with $40,000; then "Good Life U.S.A., Middle American Style" with $20,000; "Comfortable" with $15,000; "Getting Along" with $9,500; "Having a Hard Time" with $6,000; and, last in the layers was "Poverty" with only $5,700.

Now I must admit that I was more than somewhat shocked to hear that Americans are class conscious. I've always thought of my fellow citizens as otherwise. Reading further into the report, I found that all the surveying was done around Kansas City and Boston. Just to make sure the Harvard-MIT results were typical, I decided to do a little survey of my own among Americans temporarily living and working here in Tokyo.

My research wasn't nearly as thorough as the job done in the U.S. In fact, I could only corner three other Americans one afternoon after a Chamber of Commerce luncheon. Still, the results remarkably matched those of Harvard-MIT. And none of my three Americans, by the way, were from either Kansas City *or* Boston.

There was only one big difference in my survey. Because, what with overseas cash allowances and all the other perks and benefits associated with being posted in Tokyo, all three of my respondents agreed that it's impossible to figure out your own actual annual income here — much less some other American's take-home. So, my people answered the questions purely on the basis of observed life style of transplants here in Japan.

They classed the "Success Elite" — Tokyo version — as an American who has a car and a driver and one who even lets his wife use the car and driver now and then. He also has a maid, paid for by the company, and has his rent and utilities paid by the company, too. He belongs to all the best — and only — Clubs in town, and the company pays all the dues and all the club chits. He gets Home Leave every year, has melon for breakfast a couple of times a week and eats grapes for dessert on Sundays. "Success Elite" smokes as much now as he did before the prices went up last year, and he drinks Johnny Walker Black when he's home alone as well as serves it to his guests. He also works for a company that invites wives out to the evening expense account dinners.

"Doing Very Well" — next in the Tokyo class layers — was described by my respondents as one who also has a car and driver, but whose wife *never* gets to use it. He, too, has a maid, but he pays for her. His company does pick up the rent, but not the utilities. Generally, he lives in an apartment, however, where the company can't tell where the rent ends and the utilities begin. The company pays only the club dues and he even belongs to a golf club that's as close as an overnight trip from Tokyo.

"Doing Very Well" only gets Home Leave every two years, but goes to Hong Kong with his wife in the off years even if he *doesn't* win free tickets at a school dance. He has melon for breakfast only on Thanksgiving and never *did* smoke. His guests get Johnny Walker Black, but he drinks only Suntory Gin when he's alone. The company *never* invites the wife.

"Good Life U.S.A., Middle American Style" has a car but drives it himself. He has no maid, but since his wife doesn't teach English or study Ikebana, she has time to do her own cleaning. He belongs only to a health or exercise club and pays for it all himself. He gets no Home Leave, but sneaks his wife along now and then on business trips to Seoul or Taipei. He gives Johnny Walker Black only as gifts. Both to guests and by himself, the drink is gin or vodka. He does have a Japanese friend, however, who can get him things at the PX and commissaries.

141

Next layer is "Comfortable." He, my respondents decided, has no car, but knows key taxi words like "Hidari," "Migi" and "Massugu," so gets around OK. He has no maid, but the kids are big enough to do the dishes and make the beds. His wife, however, hasn't figured out how to get them to do it. He belongs only to parents' clubs at the kids' schools and doesn't like the taste of either melon *or* grapes. He only drinks when invited out to bank openings or embassy parties.

Next layer, "Getting Along," has no car, never rides in taxis, but understands subway maps and always changes at the right stations. He has no maid, but has no kids so he doesn't need one. "Getting Along" feels he's come to Japan for the entire Oriental Experience so drinks only "One Cup" Sake or Calpis, eats only Cup Noodle, soba and yakitori. He sleeps on the floor and has no utilities in his house for either he or the company to pay for. He doesn't care about Home Leave, because he's spent so much time studying Japanese that he's forgotten his native language.

"Having a Hard *Time*" — next-to-last-layer — is pegged as an expatriate who probably earns enough money to do everything "Success Elite" or "Doing Very Well" does, except for the fact that he has two or more kids in college back in the U.S. and a wife here who collects Japanese antiques and art to sell for a big profit when they get back home. His biggest single expenses here are collect calls from the kids asking for money, Sumo prints, and Imari dishes — "very old" Imari dishes.

"Poverty," after much discussion, was finally described as a former member of any of the other layers who used to be in Tokyo, but has now been transferred back home where he's once again learning to live within his means.

I have no idea how really accurate my respondents were.

On the first few layers, anyway. But, if I believe the notes on some of the Christmas cards I have received from Cleveland, they were dead center on "Poverty."

FREE ADVICE — IT'S ALWAYS WORTH IT

I've been here long enough now to be just a wee bit hesitant about giving any Japanese some advice about how he ought to run his business. That hesitancy is in spite of the fact that certain people in certain faraway places regularly remind me to start advising somewhat heavier and oftener, since that's why I was sent here in the first place.

Anyway, I'm afraid I can't resist in the case of Hiroo Onoda, the Japanese Army intelligence officer who holed up in a Philippine jungle for 30 years rather than surrender. At a luncheon and press conference held in the Foreign Correspondents' Club in Tokyo after he came home, Lt. Onoda told about some of his jungle experiences and about his plans for the future.

After listening to him — and to the answers he gave some of the questioning newsmen — I think he's going about his whole future all wrong. And, I've decided I'm going to tell him so. By the way, I was a little disappointed that he didn't say a word about any problems he had with customs or immigration at Haneda when he came back. Nor did he show us any slides of places he stayed down there. But, he did talk about business.

For instance, he says he's going to set up what he calls a small big ranch in Brazil rather than stay in Japan.

Now, for heaven's sake, he *knows* what happens to somebody who tries to go it alone in a venture in a foreign country. I mean his 30 years' experience in the Lubang jungle should have told him that — with a Philippine partner — he might have been able to make something out of his deal there.

Instead, after 30 years' working in a foreign country, he didn't even come back with the traditional gold watch. Hell, he has *nothing* to show for it — not even one cavity in his teeth.

That's another thing: Onoda-San really *didn't* have any cavities after the 30 years without fluoride, and he attributes that to the fact that he ate almost nothing but bananas all that time.

Don't you agree that, instead of the small big Brazilian ranch, he should grab some red hot Madison Avenue advertising-type and begin marketing a banana toothpaste? The possibilities are mind-blowing.

Just think of catchy slogans like: "Join the no-cavity Banana bunch." Maybe: "Don't wait until your teeth are flecked with brown and have a golden hue — brush with Banana today!" Why not: "Monkies don't have cavities; why do you?" Perhaps just: "Yes, we have no cavities."

Onoda-San, however, is passing all that up for Brazil. Mainly, he says, because he's not trained for any worthwhile job in Japan.

Maybe that's so, but he sure could hold a job that works out of Japan. He could for example, join JTB. His fellow Japanese love to travel, and he could easily map out a five-day, four-night tour to Lubang. He could show them places down there that even the Philippine Army doesn't know about. And think how cheap a five-day, four-night tour would be if Onoda-San himself worked it out. Hell, he stayed there 30 years — days and nights — for nothing!

But after listening to him, my guess is that his mind is made up and that he'll be off to Brazil as soon as he's tied up the loose ends here.

One of those loose ends I hope he'll look into is anything he might have coming under the Japanese GI Bill. I don't know how their veteran's benefits work, but I remember our World War II GI Bill entitled us to one year of college for every year we spent on active duty. If he could pass the entrance exam, that would mean Onoda-San could stay in some University or other here until the year 2005, at least. Would my kids love a deal like that!

Think about it — if he had that toothpaste deal and a dentist's degree, he'd make more money than an American orthodontist (if that's possible).

Compare all this to Onoda-San's announced plans to start up a small big ranch in Brazil. Why he doesn't even have Mitsubishi or anybody down there for his partner, much less a Brazilian. Only his brother.

Some kind of joint venture would have, I think, made more sense. But, his brother has been in Brazil for a while, so he probably can show Onoda-San where the ward office is, tell him who runs the cheapest Asian-style supermarkets, and things like that. He'll probably even be able to steer him to the right Portuguese language school.

One thing about Onoda-San's Brazilian thing *does* have some real appeal, I'll admit. That's the fact that he plans to raise about 800 to 900 head of cattle on his ranch. I don't know if that sort of thing is a real moneymaker in Brazil, but he sure could be another Onassis if he can ever get all that beef back to Tokyo.

Whatever happens, I really hope Onoda-San stays in touch and lets us know how everything goes down there. Who knows, maybe if I wind up spending 30 years in Tokyo, I might want to give it a whirl on a Brazilian ranch myself. Without my brother.

145

Of one thing I'm certain. No matter how tough things are down on the ranch, no matter how expensive bananas are, no matter what sort of troubles he has with his visa, no matter how difficult it is for him to learn the language — I'll bet he never gives up.

<hr/>

YANKEE DOODLE STILL WANTS TO GO TO LONDON

Really, I was sukoshi more than somewhat disappointed to read the results of a survey conducted some time back by the Christian Science Monitor in the United States. It seems the Monitor asked its readers: If they could choose any city at all outside of the United States to live in, which would it be? The overwhelming choice was London — picked by *over half* of the respondents.

My disappointment sprouts not from the fact that London was first choice, but because Tokyo did not even appear in the top fifty. Obviously, the Americans didn't give enough thought to their replies.

I mean, why London over Tokyo?

If it was because they like fog and drizzle, they weren't giving Tokyo a fair shake. True, we don't have much fog, but we sure have smog; and smog is so much more permanent than just plain fog. After all, fog can be burned off in no time at all by a little sunshine. Our smog, on the other hand, defies sunshine and keeps that sunshine up in the stratosphere where it belongs.

As for drizzle, why settle for only drizzle in London when you can have honest-to-Buddha rain every single day for six straight weeks every summer. And typhoons every fall — each of which brings more moisture than a decade of London drizzles.

If they chose London because of the famous Tower of London and its surrounding moat, they missed a Tokyo plus there, too. Our downtown moats around the palace have real water in them. The Tower of London's moat has only grass. And our moat's water is even greener than London's grass.

Tokyo Tower is much taller than the Tower of London, for another thing. And our Tower has a wax museum, tsubos of pinball machines, soba restaurants — everything. Is there even one pinball machine in the Tower of London? Or one bowl of soba?

Ridiculous choice.

Maybe they checked London because of the double-decker busses. That's a mistake, too. Tokyo gets more people in one-decker buses than London fits into a whole subway train.

And that's another thing: you have to get on a London subway under your own power. Have those Americans completely forgotten that, in Tokyo, the subway hires people to *push* you into the subway? Or even that people the subway *doesn't* hire push you in?

Certainly they didn't pick London because of its theaters — perfectly ordinary theaters where men play male parts and women take the female roles. They could see that sort of hokum anywhere in America, anytime. Where else but Tokyo, on the other hand, can they attend Noh theater where men play *all* the parts or Takarazuka theater where women play *all* — or almost all — the parts. Now that's worth leaving Broadway for any day.

And does the London Zoo have pandas? Even if they do, do they live in air-conditioned quarters? Not likely.

How droll it must be traveling around London where

147

Americans can read all the signs and tell the taxi driver exactly where they want to go without even handing him a map? What new frontiers can they discover with a system as simple as all that ? Why, London taxi drivers probably even *stop* every time you flag them down. Who leaves home for humdrum like that?

Chances are, Americans who go to London never catch up on their sleep, either. London impressed me as one of those wicked cities where public places stay open into the wee hours — probably even after 10:30 every night. That's trouble. I hear the movies there even start their evening shows after 7:30. God forgive them!

And even if you stay home in London, the television shows are probably all in English. After only a week or so in England, Americans can easily learn how to understand English and they'll be up half the night watching the tube. It's just not healthy to give up sleep like that.

The women, especially, would probably hate London. I mean what would they do all day? There's certainly no English way of arranging flowers or anything like Ikebana for them to study. Or doll-making. Or woodblock printing. And could they earn even one penny teaching English?

If they picked London, these surveyed Americans, because they'd get a chance to drive on the left side of the road for a change, that, too, was a mistake. In Tokyo, people drive on the left side of the road also — most of the time. But, they mix it up now and then with a little right-side driving, a little middle-of-the-road driving — sometimes they even stop at stop signs here. It's the challenge of survival that makes Tokyo driving fun, not merely different.

And in London, how could you possibly know who to smile at while you're walking the streets? I mean, everybody looks alike there, I remember. You can't tell another Gaijin from a native. That could lead to problems.

I hope it wasn't the London tea shoppes that made the Americans choose that city. If it was, they certainly aren't aware of the fact that, in Tokyo, the tea shoppes furnish free comic books to read with your tea. Or, that our tea comes in green, too.

Worst of all, what possible excuse could American businessmen in London give their home offices for less than satisfactory results? Not the language barrier. Not the culture gap. Not the lifetime employment system. Not Great Britain, Inc.

It can't be the fact that most Americans remember singing "London Bridge Is Falling Down" in kindergarten, and they want to see that Bridge. It's now in Arizona.

No, I can't understand the Americans' choice. Especially since those surveyed all now live in the United States.

Now if they had asked the same question of Americans living in Tokyo — well, that's another matter altogether.

VI. HOLIDAYS

Unless you are used to celebrating holidays like "Respect for the Aged Day," "Coming of Age Day," "Boys' Day," and some others, you'll have to learn a whole new list of holidays while you're living in Japan.

The only Japanese holiday I remember that agrees with one we had back in Cleveland is New Year's Day. The big difference, however, is that Japan celebrates New Year's Day for more than a week.

Actually, that's a much better idea. They also have a week-long holiday in spring called Golden Week. I liked that one, too.

Rather than be confused with the holiday differences, most foreigners decide to take off and celebrate both their own *and* Japanese holidays.

It's a whole new experience, and I'll share it with you.

HAPPY NEW YEAR, YOUR MAJESTY

On the second day of this New Year, we Maloneys decided that we'd go over to the Imperial Palace and pay our respects to the Emperor and his family. So, we did.

It was a truly Japanese experience. I mean the minute we came up out of the subway station at Nijubashimae, we were surrounded by those gray police trucks with loudspeakers blaring instructions about what to do next. And, just in case you couldn't hear the ones on the trucks, scores of policemen — and policewomen — were carrying portable loudspeakers.

Now I *say* these loudspeakers were blaring instructions. For all I *really* know, they were broadcasting Pepsi commercials.

Anyway, my assumption was that the Japanese people around me knew what it was all about, so we just followed them. It's maybe a 500-meter walk from the subway to the palace gate that was opened for the occasion, so there was really no danger of getting lost. Not like changing trains at Shinjuku, anyway.

Biggest danger of the day came from the New Year arrows everybody was carrying. Normally, the natives held their arrows harmlessly close to their kimonos. But, every now and then, the arrow-carriers would see something they wanted to photograph. Without warning, they would pull the camera straps from around their necks. That action caused the arrows to cut some unexpected swaths with all the threats of injuries normally only afflicted by umbrellas during the rainy season.

Thank God — and the 20th Weather Squadron — that it *wasn't* raining that day. The double-threat of umbrellas *and* arrows might have caused me to give up my palace trip and return to the comparative safety of the Tokyo subway. At least in the subway, the umbrellas are closed. All except mine, anyway. I never did learn now to refold an umbrella. And, much practice has helped me build up an effective defense against shopping bags.

Shopping bags, by the way, were a no-no in the palace grounds and one of the loudspeaker emplacements told everybody they had to check such weapons in one of the white tents near the palace entrance.

For the translation of that announcements, by the way — and for others I'll tell you about — I have to thank Son Donald. (I digress, but I did tell Son Donald again that he ought to ease off on the Nihongo lessons a little. He's missing most of the fun around here because he always knows what's *really* going on.)

Anyway, we made it through the gate. But *not* before I had my first confrontation of the New Year with the police. I was about to take a picture of the rather attractively uniformed guard at the palace gate. A policeman got into my viewfinder and said — in his own brand of English — "No pictures here; you block line. Please keep move."

Well, that made sense to me, and I smiled and kept moving. But, then I noticed a score of Japanese stopping and blocking and taking the same shot I wanted. "How come *they* can, and I can't?" I asked Son Donald.

"I don't know," he said, "because that lady policeman is saying over her loudspeaker in Japanese the same thing the policeman said to you."

"Then why are all those people taking pictures and I'm not?" I wanted to know.

"Maybe," Son Donald observed, "they are all from Osaka or Kyushu and don't understand Tokyo Japanese."

"Or," Wife Sarah chimed in, "Maybe they just object to your Kodak Instamatic."

In any event, I kept moving. Without my picture.

Once inside, we all followed the path to the palace itself. It was easy, because it was lined on both sides by plainclothes policemen. However, *all* of them had the little police department button on their coat lapels and *all* of them had that little wire that runs up Japanese policemen's necks to the tiny radio receivers in their ears. Plainclothes policemen, I notice, never carry loudspeakers.

Finally, we all reached the large courtyard in front of the window where the Emperor and his family were to appear. As the crowd collected, more loudspeakers told us — so Son Donald said — that we weren't to push toward the window and we were to be especially careful when we waved our little Japanese flags at the Emperor so that we didn't poke out any neighboring eyes that might have survived the arrows.

While we were waiting, I couldn't help but notice that windows line the entire side of the palace. My guess is that the side is 75 to 100 meters long. Inside the windows, there's a row of those sliding paper shoji doors the entire length of the building. I couldn't help but stand in awe at the fact that not one panel in those doors was torn. They mustn't allow the grandchildren inside.

Son Donald was spending his waiting time — when he wasn't translating loudspeakers — being thankful that *we* didn't live there. "My dog," he said, "would surely get lost in such a big yard."

Wife Sarah was wondering — if this were Washington, D.C. — how many people would turn out to say Happy New Year to President and Mrs. Ford and the kids.

Then, it happened. The center shoji doors opened and out came their Imperial Majesties and two of the Princes and Princesses. They waved. And we waved — hands only, we brought no flags. I heard a lot of "Banzais," but not "Happy

154

New Year." Except from we Maloneys.

In about three minutes, it was all over. Their Majesties disappeared again behind the flawless shojis.

"What do we do now?" Wife Sarah asked.

"The loudspeakers are telling us," Son Donald assured. "Follow me."

JULY FOURTH THANKSGIVING DAY?

You've probably already read or heard somewhere that this new year of 1976 — in the Oriental version of the calendar, anyway — is the Year of the Dragon.

But even more important for expatriated Americans — despite their temporary Tokyo location — is the fact that 1976 is the year of the American Bicentennial, the 200th Birthday of the United States. And so, we'd better start thinking of ways to celebrate. I, for one, am really not sure, however, how we ought to go about it.

Probably we could start by having an Indian Night Party someplace not like other "Indian Nights" you might have been to in Tokyo, either. This time, instead of serving curry and chutney, we could offer corn and buffalo steaks. Buffalo meat is rare these days, I know, but it can't possibly be as expensive as Kobe Beef. And instead of having the ice carving in the middle of the buffet table shaped like the Taj Mahal, we could carve it like an adobe hut. We could even make it a family affair and have all the mothers bring their kids along strapped on their backs like papooses. But, come to think of it, maybe that would be too Japanese.

155

And, we wouldn't charge yen to get in. Instead, everybody would have to give the doorman a handful of beads.

As part of the floor show that night, we could all bus down to Tokyo Bay and watch the committee — dressed like Indians, of course — throw green tea in the harbor to protest taxation without translation.

For the door prize of the evening, we could pull a real switch and, by telephone or somehow, award two round trips to Tokyo to somebody *from* Hong Kong.

As part of the promotion for the affair, we could sell ancient hand-made Indian pottery and rugs in the lobby area. It wouldn't cost much to set up something like that, because we could borrow the tags that say "very old" and "very, very old" from the Oriental Bazaar, I'm sure.

Maybe we could even fly in some real Indians from the Western United States for the evening. Although, come to think of it, that's maybe not a good idea. They might do a rain dance and that's the *last* thing we need in Tokyo.

Besides, there are no feathers left around here for their costumes. They were all cut up to attach to the arrows up in Meiji Shrine for New Year's.

Perhaps we'd better forget all about the Indian Party idea. We really shouldn't be glorifying them, anyway. After all, if they would have *kept* Manhattan instead of selling it for $24, all of America would be in better financial shape for its birthday party.

But, still, we have to do something to mark the anniversary. Maybe we should schedule a Cleveland Night. That could really be fun and I'm sure Wife Sarah would agree to be Chairperson.

She never minded a night in Cleveland now and then.

Gee, we could have a Polish Buffet (not for Cleveland, but for General Pulaski) and serve coffee made from the waters of

Lake Erie. We wouldn't even have to put any coffee in the Lake Erie water — unless some people like theirs light. I'm sure we could get the Mayor of Cleveland to come and be our guest of honor. The voters have been suggesting he go *somewhere* ever since the last election.

The Grand Prize at the raffle that night could be a week's vacation in Cleveland and second prize, two weeks in Cleveland.

On second thought, however, that puts us right back where we started. Any baseball fan knows that Cleveland is the home of the Indians.

Anyway, keep thinking about it. We really have to do something special for America between now and England's Thanksgiving Day.

That gives us only till July 4.

ONE OF THOSE DAYS

It was one of those days. You know the kind I mean — where everything aggravating that goes on here seems to be aimed directly and personally at me alone. I'm sure Japan has given you your share of such days, too.

You've had at least one of those days, I'm sure — like I did a couple of weeks ago — when you wonder about a whole lot of things that go on around Tokyo.

Like, for instance, have you ever wondered why the glue the Japanese use to hold the tops of milk cartons together is so effective, but the glue they put on their envelopes *never* seems to hold the back flap down? When you try to open the milk carton, you invariably tear it, the glue doesn't give. Yet, the envelope flap glue is usually licked off when you moisten it so you have to close the envelope with Scotch tape.

Or how about the political candidates, during the recent election campaigns, that rode around Tokyo for weeks promising if elected — among other things — to cut down noise pollution in our city. They made such promises, of course, from blaring loudspeakers at all hours.

Or how is it that this country came up with trees that annually burst into such beautiful cherry blossoms but sprout *no* cherries? It's a shame, because that's why bars have to put those plastic cherries in my bourbon Manhattans.

Another continuing source of wonder for me is why drivers of hired cars have to keep their motors running all the time they're parked.

Like I'm sometimes convinced that the only time that little old lady comes in to mop up the men's room is when I'm in there. And I'm left with only the Japanese-style toilet because our Japanese staff are using all the Western-style ones. Like the only time the ''yaki-imo'' man comes around at a late hour hollering about his sweet potatoes is when I've decided to go to bed early. And when I want to sleep late in the morning, that's the day the man with the little truck and the big loudspeaker does our street looking for old newspapers.

Anyway, the latest edition of ''one of those days'' started out with Daughter Barbara wanting to be driven to Sophia University in time to catch an 8 a.m. charter bus for a class ski trip. Normally, I don't consider 8 a.m. an ungodly hour, but this was on a day I planned to sleep late. So I drove her up to the school, raced back home and jumped back into bed. As I hit the pillow, the phone rang. Daughter Barbara. She had misread the flyer about the ski trip. It was the right day OK, but the bus left at 8 p.m., not a.m., and please come back and pick her up.

One of those days, all right.

I finally got back to bed, but later had to get up to go down to the ward office for a new alien registration — a perfect chore for "one of those days."

While I was showering for my ward office visit, I noticed a callous on my right foot and decided to shave it off with a little callous knife I picked up some years ago for such emergencies. It came off, I thought, without incident. But a few minutes later, while putting my socks on, I felt a sharp pain — a very sharp pain — in the foot where the callous used to be. My God, I thought, I've cut a nerve or something. But then I decided it was just a bad cramp and leaped up to see if walking around would ease the pain.

It got worse.

I sat back down and pulled off the sock, thinking I was bleeding or something. And out of the sock came the biggest bumblebee I've ever seen! Obviously, he had got in there when Wife Sarah hung the sock out on the line, had lived there for a few days, was somewhat annoyed when my foot intruded, and told me so with his stinger.

One of those days.

Anyway, I stretched out on the bed again, turned on FEN, and decided to spend the rest of that morning lying right there where little more harm was apt to come. To hell with my alien registration. Deportation, I decided at that moment, would be doing me a favor.

But, right after the FEN announcer forecast rain for "Yokuuuuuuska" — it's right near Yokosuka I think — I heard him say something about how it wouldn't be long until New Year's Day.

Could it be, I wondered, that another year was really almost over? A quick look at the day-date on my watch ended the wonder. And, it also ended one of those days and started a much brighter one.

For me, anyway, if not for those poor rained-on souls down in Yuuuuu-know-where.

Because, it reminded me of all those natives here that I wanted to send New Year's postcards to, and why I wanted to send them.

Like to the little girl in the soba shop near our office who pretends to understand my Japanese when I order Kamo-namban soba. I know now of the pretense, because the other day I ordered Mori soba and she brought me Kamo-namban. But, for months she made me feel like a true linguist.

And I wanted to write something special on the New Year occasion to that delightful man at Window No. 7 down where Tokyo people have to go to get or renew a driver's license. Window No. 7 is marked ''For Foreigners Only'' and so he knows from the start every morning that he faces nothing but Gaijin problems all day long. He, nevertheless, keeps smiling through it all and makes getting that license the nicest thing about driving in Japan.

Some cards have to go to those girls in the Ginza and Shinjuku department stores, too — the ones who wipe the escalator hand rails and say ''Welcome'' to me. Even when I'm coming to exchange something.

The Shinkansen conductors deserve a New Year Card, too. Very often — when the Shinkansen trains are running, anyway — I find myself down in Osaka or Nagoya late in the day without a reservation back to Tokyo and all the trains sold out. But, I buy a platform ticket, get on the train without an assigned seat, and always — thanks to those conductors — wind up with a seat and a smile.

There are easily a dozen police boxes around town that I wanted to send cards to in order to express appreciation for updating ancient maps given me by Gaijin friends and helping me get to the parties before the cocktail hour is over.

I even planned to include on my list the subway pushers and those old ladies with the lethal shopping bags and furoshikis. Sure they shove me around and stab my legs with those sharp corners — but never without a ''Sumimasen.''

But like the streets around town, these people have no names that I know of, and so I'll have to skip the cards.

It's too bad, too. Because their collective kindness to outsiders like me make for countless great days in Tokyo compared to the number of ''those'' days.

<hr>

YES, VIRGINIA, THERE IS A MT. FUJI

Now and then, you may have noticed, people write letters to the editor of The Japan Times and express their opinions about some of the things I have written in this space. And, you've probably also noticed, some readers don't necessarily agree with my observations one sukoshi bit.

But, that's OK. After all, you don't start off being born and brought up around New York, aging in Cleveland, and culture-shocked in Tokyo, without developing a skin somewhat thicker than an average slice of sashimi — if only in the interest of pure survival under that assortment of circumstances.

However, I must admit that sometimes a little tear comes to one eye or the other when somebody asks the aforementioned editor why Maloney doesn't go home if he hates it so much here. The tear is not for me — I *know* why I don't go home — but for the letter writers who unfortunately cannot see that I'm having the time of my life in Japan and so can't share it with me. Sure I relate stories of the everyday frustrations that we Maloneys — and most other Gaijins here — face in our daily attempts to cope. But that's where all the fun comes from. And I'm laughing at me, not at the Japanese — most of whom seem quite well adjusted to life in Japan.

The biggest bulk of the mail received, by the way, comes directly to me, and not to the editor. It takes a great deal of time now and then, but I try to answer every one.

One special such letter arrived just last week — a day or two before Christmas. Because it very closely resembled a letter that a little girl wrote to a New York newspaper about 80 years ago asking whether or not Santa Claus really exists. I thought it might be appropriate to answer it right here for everyone to see. I hope you agree with that decision — you non-letter writers, anyway!

I've suggested now and then, I guess, that Mt. Fuji, like Santa Claus, might just be an old Oriental legend concocted by old woodblock artists. And so, I have a slight touch of guilt because this little girl even felt it necessary to write such a letter.

Here's her letter — and my reply — which I hope will help settle her doubts this holiday season:

Dear Mr. Maloney:

I am eight years old.

Some of my little friends say there is no Mt. Fuji.

Papa says, "If you can get Don Maloney to say there is, then it's so."

Please tell me the truth, is there a Mt. Fuji?

Hopefully,
Virginia Gaijin

* * * * * * *

Dear Virginia:

Your little friends are wrong; they have been affected by the smog of the Economic Miracle. They think that nothing can be which is not comprehensible by their little minds. All minds, Virginia, whether they be Gaijin or Japanese, are little. In this great Kanto Plain of ours, man is like a mere cockroach that your mother has in her kitchen, a Japanese beetle, in his intellect, as compared with these boundless islands around him, as measured by the intelligence capable of grasping the whole of truth and knowledge.

Yes, Virginia, there *is* a Mt. Fuji. It exists as certainly as the empty beer cans and obento boxes that cover it exist and you *know* they abound on *all* public property. Alas, how dreary our Oriental world would be if there were no Mt. Fuji! It would be as if there were no Gaijins. There would be no Kinokuniya then, no Oriental Bazaar, no alien registrations, no gomen-nasai letters to make tolerable this existence. We should have no enjoyment except in soba or sushi. The eternal light which shines in the ward office would be extinguished.

Not believe in Mt. Fuji! You might as well not believe in multiple-entry visas! You might get your papa to hire men to watch toward Hakone every day from every tall building, but even if they did *not* see Mt. Fuji on the horizon, what would *that* prove? Nobody sees Mt. Fuji, but that is no sign that there is no Mt. Fuji. The most real things in this world are those that neither Gaijin nor Japanese can see.

Did you ever see a golf club in the hands of men who are practicing swings while waiting for the bus or for the light to change? Of course not, but that's no proof that the golf clubs aren't there. Nobody can conceive or imagine all the wonders there are unseen and unworkable — like Japanese folding umbrellas — in this world.

163

You can tear apart a mixed sandwich and see the cucumbers inside, but there is a haze covering the unseen world which not the strongest pollution laws, or all the countries in the world could tear apart. Only the extended holidays like Golden Week or New Year's or an occasional typhoon can push aside that curtain and view and picture the supernal beauty and glory beyond the Fifth Station. Is it all real? Ah, Virginia, in all this archipelago there is nothing else real and abiding.

No Mt. Fuji! Thank MITI it lives, and it will live forever. A thousand years of the dragon from now, Virginia, nay *ten* times *ten* thousand years of the dragon from now, it will continue to live — on picture postcards, anyway — and to make glad the heart of every Japanese and every believing Gaijin.

Sincerely,
Don Maloney

GOOD NEWS, BAD NEWS

The summer is just about over. And, I still haven't really decided whether it was a good one or bad one. My recollections are full of mixed emotions.

For instance, we went back to the United States in early June for Daughter Frances' wedding. It was a great affair and the fond memories will linger on, I hope, as long as the payments on the loan that financed it.

The rainy season in Tokyo ended right on time, but I

was still a little disappointed. Because it ended on the same day that I finally learned how to correctly fold up one of those supposedly foldable Japanese umbrellas. I was happy to see that my dollars each bought almost 300 yen again this summer, but saddened by the fact that 300 yen couldn't buy anything.

Not even a dollar.

The fact that Son Donald was able to get away to summer camp up in Hokkaido and do some fishing was a source of joy, too. But the news that, in two weeks, he caught only one fish, about half the size of an average piece of sushi, crossed out the joy. Especially when I figured out that the one fish cost me about ¥160,000 a pound.

Daughter Barbara came back to Tokyo after her first year at the University of Hawaii. She's loaded, however, with great stories about Hawaii. She hasn't *yet* mentioned the university.

It was fun to listen to the new incoming Gaijins recite their pledges about how they're going to be good ''guests'' here in Japan and learn the language in 60 days or less and drive out somewhere different around the country every weekend. It was tear-jerking, though, to say ''Sayonara'' to the departing Gaijin crop, who after years here, never learned the language or found room for their car on any country road on any Sunday.

It was a real pleasure to ride out a whole summer in Tokyo without shaking through a single earthquake worth remembering. But, it was nervous to learn that such stillness probably means that the promised really big quake is almost here.

Even the famous Japanese Bullet Trains had a good news/bad news story. The bad news was that they began having a lot of troubles this summer that delayed many

165

trains. The good news was that they've added — to the pushcarts that roam the train aisles loaded with dried octopus and gummy rice — a new pushcart that dispenses only beer and cocktails so you won't mind the delays.

It was nice that we escaped drowning in any major typhoons for a change this summer. But, it was not so nice the way the daily hot weather caused my deodorant to fail before 10 a.m. every morning and I drowned in my own moisture.

The price of cigarettes never did go up 50 per cent as promised. That's good. The price of everything else did go up, despite the promises. That's bad.

My new book sold very well. That's good, too. But, too many buyers are lending their copies to non-buyers to read. That's very bad.

Even the trip back home for the wedding was a mixed-emotions affair. It was, of course, good to see all the family and old friends again. Even good to see the in-laws. And the Home Office crew. But, somehow, I never really feel comfortable back there these days.

Like it still seems funny to me to get in a taxi back in Cleveland or New York without a note or card or anything to hand the driver. I mean you just tell him where you want to go and he takes you there. He even talks to you during the trip. I've sat mute in Tokyo taxis for so long that I've forgotten how to talk to a cab driver.

The New York subways don't even give you a ticket. I fished in every pocket for an hour after the IRT train got me to Grand Central one day before I realized I never had the ticket in the first place.

I also felt out of place at my favorite McDonald's hamburger stand back home. You eat your Big Mac and milk shake at a little counter there instead of off the chrome

166

garbage can, the way you do at Ginza.

I must confess, however, that I do feel more equal back in Cleveland. Mainly because everybody there pays the same prices in the same supermarkets. Nobody I know of in Cleveland has a friend who can pick up things at a PX for him.

Like I said in the beginning, the summer is nearly over. And the more I think about it, the more I'm deciding that it was a rather good one, indeed. The good news really did outweigh the bad news.

I hope you can say the same. And I hope you're ready for the inevitable frustrations that will grab you during the coming fall and winter.

Anyway, it feels good to be back in Tokyo again.

But come to think of it, maybe *that* good feeling is bad news.

VII. THE REAL JAPAN

△ 1 2 3 4 5 6 7 8 9 10 11 12 13 14 15 ▽

△
o
o
▽

After you realize that you're going to live in Japan, it's perfectly normal to study all about Japan and learn everything you can about your new home before you get here.

But, once here, you find out that it's nothing like you expected. Not because the books lied — they didn't. But, they left so much out. And, it seems, the things they left out have to do with the little daily confrontations you can't avoid and are not ready for.

Maybe it's something as simple — simple? — as learning to get around in a country where they don't give names to any streets.

Or, as complicated as trying to enjoy what the Japanese enjoy.

You'll never find the "Real" Japan, but you'll have the time of your life looking for it. We certainly did, and that's what the next few stories are all about.

WHY DON'T THEY NAME THE STREETS?

We had more than the average winter crop of Home Office visitors at our office a couple of weeks ago. While my secretary was writing out one of the dozen or more "give-this-to-the-taxi-driver" notes she put together for the visitors, one of our Cleveland people asked, "Why don't they just name the streets and number the houses and buildings like we do in Shaker Heights?"

Now I had no idea at the time why they don't. I could only assure my visiting fireman that the natives here don't do *anything* the way *anybody* does it in Shaker Heights. With one possible exception: McDonald's in Tokyo gives you a straw with a thick shake just as McDonald's does in Shaker Heights — and I haven't yet met anybody here (or there) who can suck up a single mouthful of thick shake through one of those straws.

For days after the visitors left from Haneda with their pearls and Nikons, the question haunted me. Why, indeed, don't they name the streets? Finally, I decided to ask an old Kamikitazawa neighbor of ours. He is my official Japanese folklore expert.

"The answer to that," he said, "is very simple, Maloney-San. We Japanese like our privacy."

"But how," I asked, "do people find you?"

"They don't," he answered, "and that's how we Japanese keep our privacy."

"I don't understand," I admitted.

"Oh, yes you do. In Cleveland, you tell somebody you live on Clifton Road, 18149 Clifton Road, to be exact, in Lakewood. Or, you don't even *have* to tell them; they can look

170

you up in the telephone book. With that little piece of street and number information, anybody — even a taxi driver — can find your house.''

"That's right," I agreed.

"Here in Tokyo," he went on, "I can tell anybody my address. Even give them my card with the address and numbers printed on it. But, unless I draw him a map, he'll *never* find me."

"So you draw him a map, don't you?" I asked.

"Only if I want him to come to my house. Otherwise, *only* the card."

"But surely if they really tried, they could find your house."

"I don't know, Maloney-San. Certainly *your* visitors couldn't find me. You have to meet them at Haneda Airport or they might not even find Tokyo."

"Now wait a minute, Kimura-San," I interrupted. "I never said that."

"Then why do you always go out there to meet them? Do they meet you when you fly back to Cleveland?"

"That's different."

"So is Japan. *No* map — *no* visitors. *No* visitors — *privacy.*"

Next day, in the office, I decided to pursue this particular "why don't they" question with one of our Japanese staff. Not that I wasn't satisfied with Kimura-San's answer, but I just wanted to make sure.

"Why do you ask?" my office friend wanted to know. "Do they name the streets back in Cleveland?"

"Certainly they do," I assured him.

"What do you call them?" he wanted to know.

"Well, there's Euclid Avenue, Central Avenue, Main Street, Northfield Road. . .''

171

"Wait a minute," he busted in. "What's the difference between a street, an avenue, and a road?"

I thought a second. "No difference, really."

"Then," he asked, "Why don't you call it Central Street and the other one Main Avenue?"

"That would be stupid. Central just *goes* with avenue and Main *goes* with street. Just like Sandy *goes* with lane."

"What's a lane?"

"It's another name for a street."

"Why not just call them all lanes?"

"Because you can't. Every town has a Main Street. I never heard of a Main Lane in America."

His eyes were getting wider. "I don't understand." He fretted. "If every town has a Main Street, how do you know you have the right one?"

"There's only one Main Street in each town, for heaven's sake," I told him. "And each one is different."

"Then why do you call them *all* Main Street?"

I was beginning to lose my Occidental temper. "Look," I said as calmly as possible under the circumstances, "I'm asking *you* why *you* don't name *your* streets. Answer *that* first, *then* let's talk about why we *do* name ours."

"OK, OK," he said softly. "It's just that I can't understand why anyone would want to name streets or roads or whatever they are." He was puzzled. "Don't you get your mail delivered in Tokyo?"

"Of course I do."

"And does your Tokyo street have a name?"

"Of course not."

"Then," he asked, "Why *should* we name the streets?"

"I'll tell you why," I said, "In Cleveland, when somebody asked me where I lived, I'd just simply say '18149

172

Clifton Road.' Here, I have to say, 'You know where Meguro Station is? And do you know how when you come toward Roppongi from the station, you pass under the highway? And then there's a big bowling alley on the right? Well, we're on the next street after the bowling alley on the right. Fourth house in from the main street'.''

"Hold it," he waved. "If the people in Cleveland don't happen to know where Clifton Road is, then what do you tell them?"

"I just tell them that surely they know where the shoreway is near the center of town. Well, they go west from town for a few miles, then turn left where there's a 'V' in the road. The fourth house from the corner then is . . . Oh, NEVER MIND.''

"Never mind?''

"Yes, never mind," I said. "I *know* why you don't name the streets.''

A LITTLE WOMB MUSIC, MAESTRO

Surely you read a story in the papers recently about the Japanese doctor who made a very special record for mothers to play when their newborn babies cry. The record reproduces the very same sounds a baby hears when it's still in the mother's womb. These familiar noises will calm the baby immediately, the doctor says, and the crying stops.

Anybody who has left the comparative familiarity of his hometown back in wherever to take up temporary residence in Japan knows, of course, how newborn babies feel and why they cry.

Because like the newborn baby, the brand new Gaijin is fresh out of the womb. And, again like the infant, he can't speak a single word of the out-of-the-womb language; in the Gaijin's case here, Japanese. He points to things he wants just like babies do, too.

I bet you're thinking that it would be a great idea to come up with recordings of various hometown sounds that Gaijins could play when the cultural going gets rough. Even that maybe the various embassies around town could stock cassettes of back-home noises that those same Gaijins could borrow when they feel the tears coming on.

Well, forget about it. It won't work. Not for long, anyway.

Even the Japanese doctor freely admits that the womb records only calm the babies until they're about a month old, at most. And if you can't fool month-old babies, you can't fool transplanted Gaijins, either.

In fact, one of the more annoying kinds of frustration for newcomers invariably is the sort that hits them right after they mistakenly think they have been successful in moving a little corner of home to their new little corner of Japan.

Like I was talking on a new-to-Tokyo foreigner — a New Yorker — just the other day about banks. It seems he was thrilled to death to discover that so many New York banks — including the very one he did business with back there for years — have branch offices in Japan.

Even before he made his first visit to his new office, he stopped in at the old familiar bank to open a checking account. And to do so, he went through an old familiar ritual.

He signed all the little white cards, picked out blue for his check color, made his initial deposit, then left with the bank's promise that his checkbook would be mailed to his house.

Just like home.

Just like home until the checks arrived, anyway. Because

with the checks was a letter that — so help me — read *exactly* like this, word for non-womb word:

"On request of your checkbook of our bank, I printed it. But I am sorry to mistake the printing B-check (51 sheets), instead of G-check (30 sheets) you requested. Now I enclose B-checkbook. If being troubled, please request us G-checkbook again."

Listening to his story about the old familiar bank and then the unfamiliar letter took me back to my first-ever Japanese hot dog. I was at a baseball game in Tokyo. A young man was moving thru the stands with a big box strapped around his neck just like other young men did back in Cleveland's Municipal Stadium during the Indian games.

Not only did he look the same, but he was yelling "Hot Dogs." Well, actually he was yelling "Hotto Dogu" — but with all the cheering it sounded almost the same. So, I held up two fingers, just as I would have back in Cleveland. And the others in my row passed the hot dogs along our row to me and passed my money out to the Hot Dog boy. Again, just like Cleveland.

He even included two little plastic packs of mustard. How's that for womb stuff?

But, the first bite shattered all the nostalgia. The mustard was that hot Chinese Dristan thing that does more to clear out your sinus cavities than it does to flavor the Hot Dog.

And it wasn't a Hot Dog, either; it was indeed a Hotto Dogu, just like he yelled. It was at that instant that I first realized what the Japanese do with their whales.

The womb dream ended, just like it does for the month-old baby.

But, that was four years ago. Now, I'll tell you the truth, I like those Tokyo ballpark Hotto Dogus. I even like the mustard.

In fact, not only does it taste good now, but I haven't had a sinus headache since that first mouthful.

It's a scary thought for you newcomers, I know, but I guarantee you that soon you'll be quite familiar with your new Japanese womb. Soon, the thing that will scare you most is the thought that someday you'll be returning to the old womb which you'll realize isn't the familiar one anymore.

And, just for good measure, I'll tell you something even scarier: I understand exactly what the bank is trying to say in that letter.

One day, you will, too.

※※※※※※※※※※※※※※※※※※※※※※※

TOKYO HAS ITS UPS AND DOWNS

During your first days in Japan — if you in any way resemble a normal Gaijin person — you're bound to get up-tight about some of those everyday differences here that are usually referred to as "cultural shocks."

Whether these shocks register two, four, seven, or even more on your own personal cultural Richter Scale depends entirely upon you. I mean one man's two is often another man's seven.

And, how long your personal scale goes on registering these shocks is up to you, too, I guess. For some, one jolt does it. For others, the after-shocks go on for years.

I know one guy, for instance, who's been here since MacArthur but still stiffens when natives rush into an elevator at the same instant he's trying to get off.

But, I know another who's only been here three weeks and

never passes up an opportunity to ride an elevator in Japan because he thinks it is one of the more fascinating Oriental adventures.

Now I had one of those once-in-a-Tokyo-lifetime opportunities the other night when I wound up at the St. Mary's School Annual Dance with both of these elevator people at the same table.

The subject of elevators came up — I made certain it did — and here's how it went from there:

The ''Old Japan Hand'' struck first. ''What really annoys me,'' he fumed, ''is, when the elevator you're in arrives at your floor and the door opens, the masses come charging into the elevator before you can possibly find your way out. I feel like the fabled carp — swimming upstream. Why can't they wait until I get off? Even on the subway, the incomers wait until the outgoers are off. Almost off, anyway. Why not on elevators?''

''You really don't know?'' the three-week wonder asked him.

''No, I really don't know.''

''Well,'' the newcomer volunteered, ''I figured it all out and it goes like this: First off, recall if you will, exactly what goes on in a normal Japanese elevator. Somebody always assumes the roll of operator, right? I mean, they stand over by the row of push buttons and decide when the 'Door Open' and 'Door Close' buttons should be hit and they take orders for floors.''

''That's right,'' the OJH agreed.

''If a self-appointed operator has to get off before the elevator gets all the way to the roof or the basement — depending, of course, on which way you're headed — another passenger immediately assumes command, so you're never in a ship without a captain.''

''That's right,'' OJH again agreed. ''But I'm not talking

about the people already in the elevator, including the button manager, I'm talking about the others who charge in."

"I know, I know," the newcomer assured the OJH. "I'm getting to them. Now you know there's a self-appointed operator in every Japanese elevator and so do those people who are waiting to get in at the next floor."

"So?" OJH shrugged.

"So, they know that at the instant the last leaver gets off the elevator, self-appointed is going to mash that 'Door Close' button."

"I get it now. So they are trying to get on the elevator before the last exiter gets off and the unlicensed operator closes the doors."

"*Exactly.* Try this yourself sometime: Wait until everybody gets off an elevator that stops on your floor, and then try to get in. Odds are better than even that you'll have to wait for the next elevator."

"OK — So now I understand," OJH admitted. "But isn't there some way we can change it? Can't we keep the self-appointed operators in a purely passenger role?"

"The only thing I can think of," the newer expatriate said, "is to remove all the 'Door Close' buttons from Japanese elevators. Then, there would be no raison d'etre for an operator."

"Do you believe there's really a chance that Japanese would stand for elevators with no 'Door Close' buttons?" OJH dreamed.

"I think there's as much chance of that as there is that they will someday name all the streets in Tokyo."

"That's what I was afraid of."

"Look," the newcomer asked OJH, "if elevator-riding gets you so uptight, why don't you just ride the escalators and stay away from those vertical vehicles?"

"Because," OJH sighed, "escalator manners are even harder for me to take."

"Why? What goes on on an escalator worth fretting about?"

"Well," OJH admitted, "the real reason I hate Tokyo department store escalators is not really manners, but because I hate prejudice."

"Prejudice?" the newcomer asked, *"What* prejudice?"

"I'm left-handed," OJH pointed out.

"What has that got to do with it?" the newcomer asked.

"Everything," OJH proudly replied. "Notice, next time you're in a department store, that the girl only wipes off the *right* handrail."

At this point, it was already one in the morning and the St. Mary's Dance was over. I excused myself and headed down, with Wife Sarah, to the Hilton garage for my car.

"Why," Wife Sarah asked, "are we walking down the stairs instead of taking the elevator?"

In the middle of my answer to that question, I suddenly wished all Gaijins were equipped with a "Mouth Close" button.

<hr />

PRESENT IMPERFECT

Before I ever laid eyes on Tokyo, I don't remember reading anything in American papers about Japan since World War II ended.

But, now that I'm an "Old Japan Hand," it seems that every time I go back to the United States, some Japan story or other is on page one of any paper I pick up. Even the Cleveland

179

Plain Dealer, who I don't think even mentioned Japan during World War II.

This summer, it was no different. First morning I was there, in fact, a story headline said, "Japan to Match Statue of Liberty." That story went on to say that the Prime Minister of Japan had appointed this special committee to choose an appropriate gift for his country to give to the United States as a Bicentennial birthday present. And, he was quoted as saying something like he wanted this gift to have "the magnitude of the Statue of Liberty" which France gave the U.S. when America celebrated its 100th Anniversary.

There was absolutely no hint in the story about what such a gift might be. And, of course, my imagination ran wild.

Maybe, I thought, it would be a giant Torii Gate straddling San Francisco Bay. A gate with a plaque that read "Give me your Toyota's, your Sony's, your Nikon F4's. . ." or something like that.

No, Wife Sarah thought. Too commercial. And, too real.

Then I decided the gift should be one of Tokyo's Yamanote Line railroad trains. They could circle it around Disneyland instead of that old steam engine train they have now. The cars are a little smaller on the Yamanote trains, but Disneyland would still be able to handle eighty-five times as many people as they handle now if the pushers went with the trains.

Wife Sarah squashed that idea, too, by pointing out that the only reason Tokyo fits in its 12 million people is because three million of them are always packed into the Yamanote Line trains.

Maybe, I decided, the Japanese will plan to help ease the energy crisis in the U.S. and give America all the gray busses they have — as a basis for an American mass transportation system. After all, they just park those busses in front of the government offices and embassies now. They don't take anybody here anyplace, it seems.

Again, Wife Sarah nixed it by pointing out that the entrance and exit doors on those busses are on the wrong side for America.

Finally, I gave up and decided to await the consensus of the appointed committee.

Right after returning to Tokyo, that consensus result was on the front page of The Japan Times. They had decided, the Times said, that the gift would be a 500-seat theater in the Kennedy Center in Washington and a cherry tree park somewhere on the West Coast.

Now, normally, I don't get involved in government deals like this. But, in the case of such a gift, I want to make it perfectly clear that I believe the United States should turn those presents down. At least until they completely understand what the gifts really mean.

For instance, the West Coasters — before they accept — should be told that Japanese cherry trees produce no cherries. I'd hate to have them accept on the thought that they'd be able to hold a cherry pie festival in the park every year. And, when they bloom each year, JTB will send thousands of flag-following tours to view the blossoms.

And Washington should be made well aware of exactly what Japanese think is ample accommodations for 500 people. I mean their idea of a 500-seat theater would, I'm sure, be only as big as one of those gray busses I mentioned earlier. Maybe smaller.

Besides, if they build that theater according to the same specifications that they follow when putting seats in Tokyo theaters, only those Japanese JTB tour groups would be able to sit down there. I remember that I once finally managed to squeeze my rear into a local theater seat in Tokyo. Just before the show started, I bought an ice-cream sandwich from one of those ladies walking up and down the aisle. Because I ate that sandwich, I had to stay in that seat for two days.

What I'm trying to say is that it's OK with me, these gifts, as long as the Americans know exactly what they're getting. Sort of OK, anyhow.

Actually, after reading that first Statue of Liberty story, I'm a little more than somewhat disappointed about the theater and the cherry trees. And I hardly slept the night I read about it. Not that I expected something more expensive — just something more spectacular.

Like that Torii Gate, or the Yamanote Line, or the gray busses.

But they're all out of the question. I finally realized that.

So I had to come up with some idea, I thought, or keep quiet about the whole thing forever.

I decided that I'd be able to think more clearly about the whole matter when I visited Mt. Fuji the next day with the family.

Then it hit me: Mt. Fuji! Why not give the Americans Mt. Fuji!

Wife Sarah, surprisingly, agreed. "Why not, indeed?" she asked. "For all they see of it here these days, nobody will even know it's gone."

❧❧❧❧❧❧❧❧❧❧❧❧❧❧❧❧❧❧❧❧

SHINE ON HARVEST MOON

One of my Japanese friends — always ready to help me better understand the culture we're all immersed in here — made it sound like a perfectly ordinary question: "How would you and Okusan," he asked, "like to join me next Saturday night for some moon viewing?"

I smiled, but didn't answer, because I was sure there was more to the question.

"Well?" he prodded.

"Well, what?" I wanted to know. "What's the punch line?"

Now, needless to point out to those of you who have been in Japan at least 48 hours, my use of the words "punch line" was rather unfortunate. It took me at least 23 minutes to explain that what I meant was that I was sure he was working up to some sort of Oriental joke and I was waiting for the humorous ending.

He assured me that he wasn't, that he was quite serious about wanting to know whether or not Wife Sarah and I would join him for a little look at the full moon due the following Saturday night.

"We'll go to the Hie Shrine," he explained. "That's right across from the Tokyo Hilton Hotel, and view the Harvest Moon together with a large crowd that gathers there every year at this time for just such an occasion. It's an old Japanese tradition."

I realized from the look on his face that he was, indeed, quite serious.

"Do you mean," I wanted to make certain, "that people are *really* going there to watch the moon? Can't they see it from their own backyards?"

"Of course, they can," he assured me. "But it's more fun to do it at the shrine. Besides, you'll get to see some typical old-time court dancing to some traditional court music. It's a once-in-a-lifetime chance for a foreigner like you."

Now I had to admit that he had me there. A few over forty Harvest Moons had shined down on me back in the U.S. and I couldn't recall *ever* getting a gang together to look at any of them — with or without music and dancing.

"Do you think that it will be clear enough Saturday night for us to see the Man-in-the-Moon?" I was stalling for time to decide whether or not I should commit Wife Sarah and myself to this "Moon Viewing."

"What *Man*-in-the-Moon?" he smiled. "What's the — I think you said — Punch Line?"

"There's no punch line; you can see a Man-in-the-Moon when it's full like it is at harvest time."

"But you Americans brought back your men from the moon months ago," he reminded me.

"Not a *real* man or men," I told him. "But the outlines of the darker spots on the moon that resemble a man."

"You're mistaken, Maloney-San. Or else the man only shows on the side of the moon Americans see. Here we see a rabbit."

"A *rabbit?*"

"A rabbit. Pounding out rice cakes, as a matter of fact."

Well, I was hooked. I had to admit that, in the entire time I'd been in Japan, I didn't remember ever really looking at the moon. And, that a trip to the shrine to see a rabbit on the moon would really be a lunar first. A rabbit pounding rice cakes, yet.

When I told Wife Sarah what we'd be doing Saturday night, our conversation that followed my announcement was much like the one above except that I now said the Japanese lines. And, we had no side-discussion over the meaning of "punch line."

We showed up right on time — with hundreds of other moon-viewers. And the old traditional Japanese music started. Actually, from the sounds, I thought the squatting musicians were just taking an exceptionally long time tuning up their

184

instruments. But when the sounds stopped, the people applauded wildly and I realized that I'd missed the first song.

The band played two or three more songs, I think. Or maybe they played the same song two or three more times. I'm still not sure because I was too embarrassed to ask my friend. The only instrument I recognized was a drum. Everything else looked like prehistoric bamboo kitchen gadgets.

The dancing started with a solo by a man — or maybe a woman — in a gold-braided kimono and a red mask. The metal ring the dancer had in one hand, I was told by my friend, really symbolized a snake and this dance is so famous because it depicts how the dancer first finds, then eats, a snake. And that's why he looks so happy during the dance. Actually, the dancer moved so slowly that I would have more easily believed that the snake bit him and that paralysis had set in.

Anyway, more songs. More dances. Two hours of them. And then it was dark. And there was the moon. And we viewed.

And while I was looking for the rabbit, I kept thinking how great it would have been if the last dance had been an Eleanor Powell-Fred Astaire tap across the stone lanterns to "Shine on Harvest Moon" played by real musical instruments. Even Kate Smith doing "When the Moon Comes Over the Mountain" would have made the evening seem like a rock and roll concert by comparison.

But, no Eleanor. No Fred. No Kate. And, *no* rabbit.

Next day, during Sunday brunch at the American Club, some Gaijin friends stopped by our table and asked us how we spent Saturday night.

I decided to be honest about it. "We looked for a rabbit pounding rice cakes on the moon while this guy danced and ate a snake."

"Wow!" they chorused. "Sounds like we missed a helluva party."

KYOTO REVISITED

Certainly you've read it somewhere or somebody has told you: If you want to see the "Real Japan," you have to go to Kyoto.

I know I've read that many times, and heard it even more often than that. And, I've been there. Again just recently, in fact.

The first time I ever Real Japaned it was right after we arrived here five years ago. On our way back from Osaka's EXPO '70 to Tokyo — presumably the "Unreal Japan" — we stopped off long enough to both Morning Tour and Afternoon Tour the old Japanese Capital City. That first trip and the recent one I mentioned affected me quite differently.

For instance, on that first trip, Wife Sarah and I decided that, since we were in Real Japan, we'd have a real Japanese meal. And, we asked our hotel's front desk to direct us to a real Japanese restaurant.

The young girl there suggested a place called Gion something-or-other (many places in Kyoto are named Gion something-or-other) and told us to order "Shabu Shabu" when we got there.

Well, we took her little note, gave it to a taxi driver, and were off. After a short trip, he pulled over and opened his automatic door. He pointed down a very narrow side street and said something. Of course, we understood not a word, but decided that it all meant two things. One, the restaurant was down that street. Two, no way would his taxi fit down that street and we'd have to walk.

So, we paid up and started walking. Soon, Wife Sarah pointed to a sign on an old unpainted building that said "Gion" in quite understandable Roman lettering. The rest of the sign was all in you-know-what, so we understood it to a slightly lesser degree than we understood the taxi driver.

We decided finally that that was the place, pushed back the sliding door, and walked in. Since there were only three pairs of shoes lined up inside the door, we knew right away that we hadn't been sent to Kyoto's most popular eating place. And right away we saw another difference between restaurants in Tokyo and Real Japan.

In Tokyo, we would have been met at the door by people yelling "Irashimase," or something similar. There, we were met by a barking dog. I said something to the dog — in English — and he must have understood because the barking stopped. We kicked off our shoes and started down a narrow hallway toward a bright room at the end.

When we arrived there, there was nothing but an old lady sitting in the middle of the room watching television. I gave her the "Shabu Shabu" order and she very nearly jumped out of her kimono. For all I know, what she answered was the same thing the taxi driver said. But, the clear message this time was that we were in the wrong place.

Just then, a younger lady walked in from another room and I said the only two words — or is it three — I knew that night: Gion and Shabu Shabu. Both women's faces lit up and the younger one motioned us to follow her. Back down the hallway we went and she handed us our shoes. Again a "follow me" motion and she went out the door and headed further down the street.

Around the first corner was a large building with "Gion" in rather large letters. Under that was "Shabu Shabu." She led us right to the door, bowed us in, and headed back home. I wanted to say something to her in the way of apology, but I had the feeling "Gion" or "Shabu Shabu" wouldn't do, so we just bowed back.

The recent Kyoto trip, like I said, was sukoshi different. I was there because I agreed to accompany a group of Sophia University students (from Southeast Asian countries) on a tour sponsored by the Asian Club for Promoting Economic and Cultural Communication.

I say "different" because I know almost a dozen or so Japanese words now and they weren't even necessary since we had bilingual guides and all the students spoke excellent English. And, we didn't even try to find a Shabu Shabu place. The excellent tour arrangements gave us no opportunity to get lost, either.

In Kyoto, on the first day, we visited the old castles and shrines and walked around the expansive gardens complete with giant crooked pine trees and ponds full of rocks and waterfalls.

On the second day of the tour, we went on to a town close to Osaka to visit the Matsushita factory where — among other things — they produce National and Panasonic radios and TV sets (one of the former every second of every day).

I leave it up to you to decide which of our days on that second trip to Kyoto was spent in the "Real Japan."

I'M THE PERSON WHO EATS

It's not possible, if you were around here at the time, for you to have missed the furor caused a while ago by a Japanese TV commercial for some kind of instant Chinese-like noodles. It seems (and I say ''seems'' because I do have to take a linguist's word for such things) that, in the commercial, a woman who appears to be the wife says ''I'm the person who cooks'' and the man — or supposed husband — says ''I'm the person who eats.''

Now the Japanese chapter of AWAOIWY (the Association of Women to Act on the Occasion of the International Women's Year) jumped all over that noodle maker and insisted that the ''discriminatory'' commercial be dropped.

That's not the *real* news however. The *real* news — to me, anyway — is that the noodle maker dropped it. And that could be the end of an era. And maybe the end of Japan as we know it.

One of the first things that interested me about this country was the obvious discrimination against women. I mean right from the time we touched down at Haneda. At what other airport arrival terminal in the world do you see the women carrying the pineapples, suitcases, and duty-free goodies while the man totes only the passports and Declaration of Unaccompanied Goods?

And even as we roamed the department stores here, I realized Japan was the only place I ever saw the women strap their babies on their backs so their hands would be free to carry the shopping bags and leave papa with both of his hands free so he could practice his golf swing until ''Don't Walk'' turned to ''Walk.''

Does all this TV noodle business mean that Japanese females are no longer going to cover their mouths when they laugh from now on? Are they going to walk right up alongside their men now instead of that respectful three-paces-to-the-rear-and-two-to-the-left?

I was shocked enough by this TV rhubarb to find out that Japanese husbands put up with instant noodles at all. I thought they demanded that their wives start noodle dinners right from the raw flour — or whatever it is that you scratch start noodle dinners from. Now these women even reject the idea of being the person who cooks *instant* noodles?

Does this mean that Japanese wives will soon balk at scaling and slicing the raw fish and make husbands eat fins and all?

If so, who will feed a Japanese husband when he comes home from a night of Mahjong with the boys or from an evening at the cabaret where he's been fed only peanuts and those shellac-dipped crackers to blunt the throat burn of local whiskies?

Heaven forbid, suppose it all spreads to the cabarets themselves and the hostesses refuse to feed the peanuts and shellac-dipped crackers to men? Or to pour their whisky and sake? Or to wipe off the customer's fingers?

Will the Japanese husband then be forced to go right home after work? And to what? To *raw* instant noodles?

Does this brewing revolution mean we are in danger of not getting our escalator handrails wiped clean any more? Is it *that* serious?

Next, the women will want to get into taxis first and go through doors first and have their chairs held at the restaurant tables and other barbarian things like that. They probably won't even pass toothpicks to their men after dinner. I really begin to shudder at the thought of what might happen if the girls in my office get wind of what AWAOIWY is stirring up. When they do, they'll probably refuse to serve green tea every hour and then ...

But then I thought a little deeper. No more green tea. Maybe there's a silver lining after all around those Chinese noodles.

No green tea, however — I further reasoned — is too high a price to pay and the blood in my chauvinistic veins returned to the boiling point.

I decided to go home and attack in case Wife Sarah had been influenced by all this noodle thing.

I walked into the house without even taking my shoes off, met her face to face and announced: "I'm the person who eats and you're the person who cooks. Understand?"

"Well," Wife Sarah reacted, "I don't know what brought all that on, but any fool can take one look at you and know without a shadow of a doubt that *you're* the person who eats. And *eats* and *eats* and *eats* and *eats*. As for me being the person who cooks, that's fine. The mess you leave around when you cook hands me five times as much work as I'd have if I did the cooking myself."

Not sure whether I was winning or not, I decided to sort of change the subject. "What's for dinner, anyway?" I asked.

"Chinese noodles," she answered.

GIVE AND YOU SHALL RECEIVE

In preparation for my business assignment in Japan, I spent many hours in the Cleveland Public Library scanning books with titles that promised they would help cushion the certain cultural shock that I understood awaited me across the Pacific.

And I have to admit the books helped — to some extent. For instance I knew I'd have to forget about shaking hands and learn to bow. I was quite aware that the native language in Japan wasn't English. And that I wouldn't even be able to read the signs.

The books very carefully spelled out all the differences in the way business — *and* pleasure — is done in Japan. And that Japanese drive on the left side of the street and that the government was a little to the right.

All of that I was ready for.

When I finally arrived here, hat and family in hand, I discovered that most of what the books said was indeed true.

But, unfortunately, I also discovered that the books left an *awful* lot unsaid. And, as a result, left me totally unprepared and cushionless for a rather wide range of those cultural shocks.

One, especially: Gift-giving.

Let me tell you how it works here — from my own experience anyway.

First off, understand that the Japanese *love* to give gifts. Actually, they *love* to *receive* gifts. But the best way to be certain of receiving a gift is to give one. That's because some old Japanese law or something requires that every receiver pay back in kind at his earliest opportunity. I can't tell you *why* it works that way any more than the books told me *why* you bow here instead of shaking hands. But that's the way it is.

Our first confrontation with the gift shock came immediately upon occupying our first house here out in Kamikitazawa, a Tokyo suburb. Now when we moved to Cleveland from New York, some of our new Ohio neighbors got together and baked a cake which they brought over and

192

presented to Wife Sarah one day. Sort of a "Welcome to the Neighborhood" gesture.

Not so in Kamikitazawa — or in anywhere else in Japan, I'm told.

Instead, I was told by my Japanese secretary, we, as newcomers to the neighborhood, had to bake cakes or buy cookies or something like that and go around and present them to our neighbors and announce our arrival.

I certainly didn't want to be the odd one on the block — any more than I already was just by being Occidental — so I encouraged Wife Sarah to do just that. And she did.

As a result of those first meetings with gifts in hand, we count those Kamikitazawa neighbors among the best friends we have anywhere in this world, although we have since moved into downtown Tokyo.

And there, of course, did the gifting all over again.

Anyway, after those first gifts were distributed, a day or two passed. Then the neighbors started arriving at our front door with gifts of their own — each much better and more expensive than the ones Wife Sarah passed around.

I chided my secretary for not telling me about that. "Good heavens," she said, "now *you* must bring gifts to those people who brought you gifts after you brought them gifts."

I was sure I misunderstood her valiant attempt at an explanation in English of a Japanese custom.

I didn't. That's the way it goes here. And, believe me, *keeps* going and going and going. Each gift bigger and better than the last.

If you don't start the whole thing by giving the first gift, the Japanese have all sorts of excuses to kick off the chain themselves.

They have national gift-giving seasons in July, in December for year-end, on New Year's day for year-beginning, plus Christmas — which I'm sure they've adopted into their culture for the gift excuse it brought.

And there are all sorts of rules involved with Japanese gift-giving. For example, the giver must always say that the gift he gives is unworthy, that it's really nothing — no matter what he hocked to pay for it.

The receiver, on the other hand, must never open the gift until the giver leaves the premises. And the next time the receiver sees the giver after that, he must thank him for his gift before he even says ''Hello.''

And, of course, give him a gift.

Little strings that go around wrapped gifts in Japan (instead of ribbons) come in many colors, or combination of colors, has a very special meaning that you have to get with to avoid disaster.

Like once when an old Japanese lady friend of the family's was celebrating her birthday, I decided on a gift certificate from a local department store. They offered to wrap it for me and I accepted. Pointing to a host of strings — red and white, gold and red, silver and gold, black and white, etc. — the clerk asked me which ones I preferred.

Because it looked the richest, I chose silver and gold.

Disaster. It *should* have been red and white.

Silver and gold, I later learned, are *only* for wedding gifts. And one of the real disappointments of that old lady's life was that she never got married. She thought I was needling her.

Speaking of weddings, you bring gifts to the bride and groom here, just like in Cleveland. But here, you also bring gifts home *from* the bride and groom. The first time that happened to me, I was shocked because the newlyweds' gift to me was more expensive than mine to them. Next wedding, I upped the value of my gift, but the one I got was *still* better. Five weddings later now, that same pattern is still in effect.

194

But my fondest memory of gift-giving in Japan is one that I thought would be the easiest to pull off.

Mind you, I said "thought."

The American Ambassador to Japan sometime back was Armin H. Meyer. Ambassador Meyer was leaving Japan for a State Department home office post in Washington. It is usual here for remaining foreigners to get together and throw a "Sayonara Party" for departing brethren. And Ambassador Meyer's party was to be hosted by the Tokyo American Club. My job, assigned by the party organizer, was to select a gift to present to him and Mrs. Meyer.

Simple. I *thought*.

The results of a rather thorough investigation at the Embassy, however, indicated that His Excellency already *had* everything that was within our means to give. No matter what idea I came up with was met with a "They have one already."

I sat pondering the organizer's charge that the gift "must be especially representative of the Ambassador's stay in Japan."

I decided on one more foray to the Embassy with one more list of possibilities. But, as I approached the Embassy gate, a whole new idea struck.

You see, certain groups of dissenters in Japan — from both the left and the right — have a tendency to express their dissatisfaction by gathering in rather ruly groups around buildings occupied by various branches of their own government — or around Embassies of foreign governments that may be involved — and carry out orderly demonstrations designed to communicate their dissatisfaction.

On occasion, these demonstrations have been known to become unruly and disorderly for some reasons or other. So, the Japanese government provides what we foreigners call "Riot Police" to stand by those buildings in case "ruly" is proceeded by "un" or "orderly" is preceded by "dis." And they're dressed for the job — in paratrooper boots, navy blue uniforms, hockey player gloves, football lineman arm padding, motorcycle helmets with plastic face-shields, and they carry a King Arthur shield and wield a broomstick.

Now, while Ambassador Meyer was here, some groups were concerned that the reversion of Okinawa was taking too long, that the war in Vietnam was lasting too long, and that the U.S. shipments of soybeans to Japan were too short — among other things. So Ambassador Meyer never left nor entered his Embassy without passing thru the "Riot Police."

And that, I decided, is what we would give him — a "Riot Policeman." Real, alive, and ready for action.

In my own straightforward way, I walked up to the police box at the gate and said, "I'd like to borrow a policeman."

"For what?" was the expected question.

"To give as a gift."

Well, the man in the box obviously thought he misunderstood me and we went on and on. Finally, he tried to end the whole conversation with an "Impossible!"

But I wasn't going to give up.

Finally, he agreed to lend all of the gear, but not a policeman. Find your own man, he told me, and send him over for the outfit. One of the other American businessmen here had a Japanese assistant and we told him our plans and how *he* was selected to play "Riot Policeman" for our gift.

The convincing discussion with him took only slightly less time than my talk with the police chief. But he gave in and I told him to go to the police box at the Embassy and pick up the outfit.

Next day, his American boss called. The Japanese assistant was more than somewhat disturbed. It seems that the chief decided that if our man was going to *dress* like a policeman, he was going to learn to *act* like one. And so he put him through hours-long basic training before turning over the outfit.

The next day at the party, I made my presentation speech to Ambassador Meyer, called for the curtains to open disclosing the giant box on center stage, and pulled the strings (red and white this time). The sides of the box collapsed and our "Riot Policeman" leaped out — broomstick and all.

I'll never forget the look on Ambassador Meyer's face.

Or that he never returned a gift.

VIII. GOING HOME

Suddenly it's over. And the reverse culture shock begins. You're going home . . . to stay.

Not that you didn't know the day was coming sooner or later. It's just, I think, that because it didn't come sooner when you would really have welcomed it, you hate to see it come later after you've learned to cope and could go on forever.

There's a lot I could say about my own personal feelings about going home, but I don't think I could say it any better now than I already did in these final stories that follow.

HOME IS THE PLACE WHERE...

You probably saw the item in one of the local dailies. It was a report of some survey conducted recently among multinational companies in the United States. These companies, the item said, listed as their No. 1 Problem the fact that they were having a terrible time getting their overseas-stationed executives to come back home.

Now I don't know about you, but I was shocked. Overseas-stationed executives that I know — all of them, of course, on duty in Tokyo — always seemed to me to be counting the days until they could jump on that Sayonara Jumbo for Cleveland or wherever.

But, that's not what the article said. So, I decided to check out some of the local overseas-stationed executives point blank. I mean I only had the impression they all were anxious to hit the hometown road, and it occurred to me that I'd never really asked them outright.

My first stop was the American Club and I slid up to a loner at the end of the Stag Bar. "Charley," I opened, "do you want to go home?"

"Why?" he asked. "Did my wife call?"

"No, no." I smiled. "Not home *here*, home *there*."

"Where's *there*? What the hell are you talking about?"

"I mean, do you want to go back to Kansas City?"

"Certainly I want to go back to Kansas City. And, when Home Leave time comes up again next year, that's exactly where we're going."

"No, Charley," I said. "Not for Home Leave. For *good. Forever.* Leave Japan and *never* come back."

"Now, why," he wanted to know, "do you ask a

200

question like that out of the blue.''

I told him about the article I was checking out.

''Surely they're talking about guys stationed in plush spots like in Paris or London or Rome,'' Charley was certain. ''They *can't* be talking about Tokyo. Everybody here wants to go home.''

I tried again. ''Do *you* want to go home?''

''Who would want to stay on in Tokyo? I mean who would continue to put up with all this if they didn't have to? Really *have* to?''

Once more: ''Charley, do *you* want to go home?''

''Good heavens, who would want to stay here with a language as complicated as this place. The way they push you around on the subways and trains?''

Again: ''Charley, do *you* want to go home?''

''Think about the outlandish rents they charge here and the prices of melons and grapes. And don't forget the taxis. *Hate* those taxis.''

''Charley . . .'' I tried, but he interrupted.

''Nobody in his right mind would hang on here where you can't understand any television and never see a football game on Sunday and where they serve you fish raw and put everything on rice and . . .''

My turn to interrupt: ''Charley, you're not answering my question. Do you want to go home?''

''Listen, I can't even fit in movie seats here. And it's no fun to drive anywhere on weekends. It rains all during June; you sweat all summer long; and when fall finally comes, the rains come back — as typhoons instead of drizzle.''

I was determined to get a ''Yes'' or ''No'' out of Charley and popped the question again.

''All that I've mentioned and I haven't even come to the earthquakes yet . . .''

201

"Look, Charley," I cut in. "Please give just a Yes or a No."

"Promise you won't tell anybody what I say?" he asked.

I promised. (Charley isn't even his real name.)

"No, I don't want to go back. Not now, anyway. The multinationals can count me in with the nays."

"But, Charley, you just gave me a dozen reasons for wanting to leave Tokyo *now —forever.*" I gasped.

"But, Charley, nothing," he snapped. "I *have* to sound like I don't like it here or I'll lose half my friends. I don't want to go home — or to Paris, either. Sure this language is tough, but I can't even say 'this is a book' in French. And, besides, the way all our wives are teaching, everyone in this country will speak English soon. I don't really care about the subways or trains or taxis, either. I've got my own car. Plus, who cares about the rent? The company pays most all of it. I never did eat grapes and melons, anyway. Biggest favor Japan gave me was to draw me away from the TV where I used to sit for 30 or 40 hours a week back home."

Charley paused only long enough to take a bite out of his club sandwich and down a couple of French Fries.

"I don't even go to the movie houses here, either. And last but not least, I'm not here when it rains; I'm on Home Leave."

Charley was still going on as I eased out the door and went up to the swimming pool to take a dip before meeting Wife Sarah at the Hilton's Keyaki Grill for dinner. I hated to leave while he was still talking, but I had to.

I was afraid Charley was getting ready to ask me the same question.

747'S THAT PASS IN THE NIGHT

Whether it's for keeps or just for the summer, previous experience here tells me that, by the end of the first week in any June, 7.2 out of every 10 foreigners in Japan will be heading for home.

And the ships — or 747's more likely — that the homeward-bound group will pass in the night will be bringing the newer crop of foreigners to Japan.

There's precious little I can say to the foreigners who are leaving. Except, of course, for ''Sayonara.'' They know what they're getting out of, or getting into, by going back home. Most returnees, I suppose, leave with an I-can't-wait-to-get-home attitude. At least they talk like that before they go.

But the great majority, I've observed, cannot hide that small tear or two that appears in the corners of their eyes as they bow their final goodbyes.

On the way to Haneda airport, they must realize that the taxi driver facing that telephone pole alongside the highway is maybe the last taxi driver they'll ever see doing what the one they are seeing is doing on that telephone pole.

And surely they've thought about the fact that probably no restaurant back home has a staff that will holler ''Welcome'' in one voice as they enter. Nor will anyone hand them a hot or cold towel along with the menu. Chances are, nobody will say ''Thank you'' when they leave the restaurant, either. Especially if they forget to tip. And there won't be any toothpicks on the table. Plus, in a home country where the streets are named and the houses and buildings are numbered, the go-homers know that all the mystery and adventure of a taxi ride will end.

They're aware, too, that they are going to hear the word "No" again. More each day than they heard it in two or three years in Japan.

The idea of going back to a land where the mother's clubs of your kids' schools will maybe never have a formal dance in a posh hotel or give away any tickets to Hong Kong must cause a certain sadness, too.

And where, the women are probably thinking, in Cleveland or Kansas City or wherever, can you kill a morning or afternoon a week learning how to arrange flowers or make dolls or play mahjong?

It begins to dawn on those same women, I'm sure, as they head back that, from now on, they'll have to find out for themselves why the electric bill's so high, or where to buy ample-size bras, or how to order something by phone. Certainly the husband's secretary back home isn't interested in offering that sort of help.

And the gals who have been using Oriental substitutes in their favorite recipes are more than likely worried about whether they'll be able to remember how to put that stew together using only the real things again. Plus no more days off for subway or railroad strikes or going to pick up the alien registration. No more holidays for the Emperor's Birthday or Boys' Day or Sports Day or anything like that.

Not only will they never wake up to a loudspeaker again, but they'll have to cook their own sweet potatoes.

The go-homers with more than the normal one or two tears in each eye are most likely those special ones who know they are not only leaving all of the usual, but also the maid and the driver.

So, you see what I mean. With all that on their minds and more, what can you say other than "Sayonara?"

On the other hand, what can you say to the new bunch of

unregistered aliens coming in?

The new women, especially, will be shocked by the taxi driver and his telephone pole routine.

It'll be a while before they even realize that what the restaurant staff is hollering means "Welcome." At least 10 per cent of them will think the oshibori towel is some sort of Japanese food and will try to eat it. They'll have no idea how to act when the waiter refuses a tip. They'll curse the presence of toothpicks and the absence of napkins.

They'll be confused — as all of us once were — when they learn that saying it louder, and even louder than that, that no taxi driver knows where to go just because they gave him what they thought was a name and address.

And they'll wonder for weeks — or maybe even for months — how come almost nothing they ask for ever happens, even though everybody says what the phrase book claims means "Yes."

And they'll take sometime to figure out why grammar schools that charge a couple of thousand dollars tuition have to have weekly fund raising events. Worse than that, they might actually win a free trip to Hong Kong and then surely find out that getting to Hong Kong and back is, by far, the least expensive part of such a trip.

But, sure as sushi is raw, these newcomers will begin to get with it. The women will start taking the lessons on how to put the flowers all over one side of the vase. The men will learn that the purpose of Japanese business meetings is not to reach decisions, but to talk about *how* to reach decisions.

In a fairly short time, the newcomers will start to praise a lot of things Japanese. And, they'll complain about a lot more things Japanese.

Eventually, they'll even start telling others how they'll be going back home again in a couple of weeks or months.

And, one day, the time will come when they really do go back home.

Then, that tear or two will come to their eyes, too.

I'll bet you a cup of green tea.

※※※※※※※※※※※※※※※※※※※※※※※※

SAYONARA!

The call was bound to come one day, and — a few weeks ago — it finally came. That home office call with one of those legendary offers that you can't refuse. And as a result, we Maloneys are about to head back to Cleveland. For keeps.

How does it feel to know that, at last, the Japan Experience is about to end?

I view the whole thing with mixed emotions. When I first came to Tokyo on a two-year assignment more than five and a half years ago, I couldn't imagine that the day could *ever* come when I could greet "we're going home!" news with anything short of a very very large *"Yahoo!"*

But the "We're going home!" news came and I've yet to hear even a very very small "Yahoo!"

Not from me.

Not from Wife Sarah.

Not from the kids.

Oh, it's not that I don't *want* to go back home. Nor is it that I want to stay in Japan forever. But for those five and a half years Japan *has* been home. And we've loved every minute of it. *Almost* every minute anyway. I must admit there was a rather trying breaking-in period.

When Wife Sarah and I made a quick trip to the U.S. last month to look for a house, I viewed Cleveland quite differently than I've ever viewed it before. There's a hell of difference in your attitude between a "home leave" trip and a "leave for home" trip.

Not that Cleveland has changed *that* much in the last five and a half years. But I'm afraid *I* have.

You still have to tip the waiters there and you still have to open your own taxi doors. Melons are still cheap there and they still practically *give* grapes away. They still drive on the right side and almost everybody you meet speaks English. It's still wrong to slurp your soup there and you still have to pick your teeth in private. Nobody there would think of paying more than seven bucks for Johnny Walker. All that's just as I left it.

But, and I don't know quite how to explain it, I just don't feel entirely comfortable there. I'm a stranger in my old hometown. And yet, I know I belong *there,* not here. For me, that's the *real* world.

Of course, looking for a house didn't help much. When we left Cleveland, we sold our house.

It was a great house — perfect. But now, we'll have to pay about a hundred per cent more for a house that we'll live in until we find something decent.

The new little cute compact cars cost as much apiece as we paid for *two* cars about a year before we left. But still, I guess we'll be able to pay for it all just by what we'll save by staying out of Tokyo's Kinokuniya Supermarket for a year or so. (But, just in case, please buy another copy of my book.)

I've decided, though, that it's not the going back to Cleveland that leaves me less than ecstatic. It's moving away from Tokyo.

It's so damned hard to get to feel that you belong here, that you can cope, that you can find your way back home from the office (and vice versa) — it seems a pity to just walk away from it all.

207

What I'm trying to get around to is the fact that I'm *really* going to miss this place. And especially the people. Not only the extremely polite, patient and understanding Japanese, but also the ''we're all in the same boat'' Gaijins.

I'm even going to miss the every-Sunday chance I've had to speak my piece here in The Japan Times. And to hear many of you speak *your* piece right back. I'll always feel good knowing that many of you have enjoyed reading this thing — although not nearly as much as I've enjoyed writing it.

But enough of that. I have to start concentrating on the *good* parts of the news about leaving Tokyo. I thought, for a brief moment, of saying ''No'' to the return home, of looking for another job with another company that would keep me in Japan. But I realize that I've already been away too long. I'm a good part Japanese now and I'm not really making the Gaijin contribution I should to our Joint Venture company. So I feel I'm cheating the Japanese. I may even be cheating my own company. I *know* I'm cheating myself.

So thank heaven I'm getting out before they open Narita airport up in Siberia and add a couple of hours more to over-the-Pacific trips. And I'm doubly happy that I'm getting out before the Japanese decide to do something silly like all learning English, or naming the streets, or putting a bunch of English-language programs on television, or make other moves that might destroy the enjoyable confusion here.

This last month in Japan will be a real problem.

Not because moving back is a real big physical chore; it isn't. The moving men will come in — the packers in the first wave — and take care of everything. That's what the letters of quotation from the moving company say, anyway.

But, despite the promises in the letters, they'll *not* do *everything.* In fact, the letters pointedly ignore the worst part of the leaving-Japan experience. And that's deciding *what* to take back with us.

Actually, I don't think it's fair for my company to pay for the moving expense. It ought to be shared equally by Oriental Bazaar and a string of antique and junk shops from Hokkaido to Okinawa.

It's *their* "very very old" things we're taking back — if Wife Sarah and I can ever agree before the packers get here.

Like the sumo prints — should they go? If so, why? Who in Cleveland will believe grown, fat men really cavort around like that in public — even on TV? Who back there will think those prints are anything other than some Japanese artist's sketches of how I dressed in my office here? Who could explain Sumo itself to a capital "G" Gaijin?

And the real, genuine, authentic, honest-to-Buddha Imari dishes.

Will anybody buy the story that we've spent a small fortune on plates that we don't dare use? Who will believe a plate could get to be a hundred years old? Certainly nobody with kids in the family.

What about the old scrolls with the tassels hanging on the bottoms? Won't they look kind of silly on plywood paneling?

I suppose we can't leave the spice jars, vases, and brass pots behind. Especially since Wife Sarah has had lamps made out of all of them.

The clock I have here on my desk — the one that tells me what time it is everywhere in the world — do I bring that home? Once in Cleveland, will I *give* a damn what time it is everywhere in the world?

There's the hibachis to worry about, too. Round ones, square ones, rectangular ones. Pottery ones, brass ones, copper-lined wooden ones. I certainly can't tell any home office people what hibachis were supposed to be used for in Japan. Not the

209

way I complained to them about how much my heating oil bills are here.

How about all the dolls we have in those glass boxes? I can't possibly suggest we leave them behind; Wife Sarah made them all in doll class. The dolls, that is, *not* the glass boxes. But, if we take the dolls, we have to take the glass boxes, too. For all I know, the dolls will disintegrate if taken out of their glass box and away from that forever little cup of water.

Then there's the stone lanterns out in what our lease jokingly calls our yard. Where would we put them in Cleveland? Not out on the front lawn. Everybody will think we've opened a Chinese restaurant. Maybe we should — it will help justify what Wife Sarah spent on Chinese cooking lessons.

All the wooly little slippers — and the rack by the front door that holds them — are *not* going to Cleveland; I'm determined about *that*. Nobody there is going to take their shoes off — even when we tell them what we spent for the Taiwan carpets. That means the six shoehorns can stay behind, too.

We'll probably have to get a twelve room house when we get back. Otherwise I'll have to hang more than one of our Oriental clocks in each room.

The tansus stay, too. One of the big plusses of Cleveland will be to have bureaus with drawers that really work. Silently.

The irony of the whole thing is that the things I'd *like* to take back, I can't.

Like Sunday brunch at the American Club. Like the American Club itself. Like *any* club where the company pays the dues. Or a television that receives only programs in Japanese so I don't get into the Johnny Carson/Archie Bunker habits again. Or my overseas allowance. Or visitors who bring me duty-free Old Grandad.

Or 110,000,000 people who get me where I'm going

every time I get lost.

But thank heaven I *can* take Wife Sarah and the kids back — *and* all the memories of the most exciting, frustrating, interesting years of my life. And, believe me, that alone is worth a million to me.

Dollars, *not* Yen.

When I made my departure announcement in the office the other day, one of our staff said his Sayonaras and then added, "Please, Maloney-San, don't *ever* forget Japan."

He's *got* to be kidding. I instead egotistically hope that Japan will never forget me.

Sayonara!

212

AFTERWORD

After six years of living, working, laughing, crying, praising and damning in Japan, I was convinced that I'd lived through everything that could possibly happen to a Gaijin in Japan.

And, in this book and in the previous one (Japan: It's Not All Raw Fish), I think I've shared all of those stories with you.

Now, after being back in Cleveland for more than nine months, and after meeting other repatriated Gaijins and listening to their stories, I know I've only scratched the surface.

What I'm getting around to is this: Certainly you have some Japan stories of your own that you'd like to share with somebody who would understand what you're talking about.

I think I'd understand, and I *know* I'd love to hear them. Next time you have a chance, how about dropping me a note and telling me your Japan story? Send them to:

> Don Maloney
> 18149 Clifton Road
> Lakewood, Ohio 44107
> U.S.A.

And, one of these days, I'll tell you all about what happens when a Gaijin comes home.

What happened when *this* Gaijin came home, anyway.

Arigato gozaimashita!

Don Maloney